||| ||||||||||||| ||| ||||||||||||||||||||||| |||
⟨⟩ **W9-ADW-345**

THE IMPORTANCE OF SCHOOL SPORTS IN AMERICAN EDUCATION AND SOCIALIZATION

Ronald M. Jeziorski, Ed.D.

Foreword by
Rev. Theodore M. Hesburgh, C.S.C.
President Emeritus, University of Notre Dame

306.483
J59i

UNIVERSIT.
PRESS OF
AMERICA

Lanham • New York • London

Copyright © 1994 by
University Press of America®, Inc.
4720 Boston Way
Lanham, Maryland 20706

3 Henrietta Street
London WC2E 8LU England

All rights reserved
Printed in the United States of America
British Cataloging in Publication Information Available

Library of Congress Cataloging-in-Publication Data

Jeziorski, Ronald M., 1945–
The importance of school sports in American education
and socialization / Ronald M. Jeziorski ; foreword by
Theodore M. Hesburgh.
p.   cm.
Includes bibliographical references and index.
1. School sports—Social aspects—United States.   2. Socialization.
I. Title.
GV346.J49   1994   306.4'83'0973—dc20   94–5788 CIP

ISBN 0–8191–9488–3 (cloth : alk. paper)
ISBN 0–8191–9489–1 (pbk. : alk. paper)

The paper used in this publication meets the minimum requirements of
American National Standard for Information Sciences—Permanence
of Paper for Printed Library Materials, ANSI Z39.48–1984.

Dedication

This book is dedicated to three men who exemplify the best of qualities promoted in school sports and other co-curricular activities. Each has had a significantly positive influence on my life and the lives of many others. With much affection and appreciation to:

Walter A. Moore -
      My high school coach, teacher, and early inspiration

Angelo Schiralli -
      My college teammate, inspiration, and compadre

Anthony Souza -
      My former player, student, inspiration, and cherished friend

N.C. WESLEYAN COLLEGE
ELIZABETH BRASWELL PEARSALL LIBRARY

Contents

·

Foreword

In *God, Country, and Notre Dame*, I wrote that sports are an important microcosm of life. Basic life values confront those involved as they must participate according to neutrally administered rules of the game in front of all to see on the playing fields and courts. In *The Importance of School Sports in American Education and Socialization*, Ron Jeziorski expands this perspective to apply to all voluntary co-curricular activities in the middle and secondary school years. In addition to identifying the value of these programs in complementing and reinforcing the classroom learning experience, he describes many other significant educational benefits of these activities to our youth as well as our nation.

Ron, as a father, former athlete and coach on the junior and senior high school and college levels, businessman and infantry officer in the U.S. Marine Corps, has had broad experience to observe how the dynamics involved and the lessons learned from co-curricular participation are helpful in preparing youth for various life roles after graduation from school. He explains how co-curricular participation involves educational experiences which help to counteract various negative influences of our contemporary society on youth: (a) instability, insecurity, and lack of direction among youth caused by divorce; (b) confusion about values fostered among youth by mixed messages emanating from the media as well as broken family relationships; and (c) the lure of gang involvement as a family proxy to satisfy many of the needs of youth that are otherwise not being met in many sectors of our nation today.

As our nation's population has become increasingly pluralistic culturally, the need for popular activities which involve people from all backgrounds on a common basis becomes more pronounced. This is especially true for youth as they develop their perceptions of others who differ from themselves culturally, religiously, socio-economically, and racially. Ron emphasizes that one of the most significant benefits of co-curricular programs is in promoting community by breaking down barriers of diversity among our youth towards the pursuit of common goals. Whereas students attend classes with members of other backgrounds by mandate, they voluntarily interact with others through participation in co-curricular programs. He argues that it is in these school activities that youth most regularly pursue individual achievement concurrently with the good of the team: the community of others to which he or she belongs.

In addition, this book describes how co-curricular programs provide youth with other valuable educational opportunities such as the constructive introduction to and practice of equitable competition which is the basis of our free enterprise economic system. One of the most important functions that citizens of a democracy should learn at an early age is the ability to strive for one's own improvement while being concerned with the good of one's community as well. Ron describes how co-curricular participation regularly provides youth opportunities to develop such interpersonal and cooperative awareness and skills. Development of these skills also help youth to prepare for later employment.

Finally, while the need for mandated classroom learning of scientific, quantitative and literacy skills is obvious in our need as a nation to keep up with if not get ahead of the rest of the world technologically, we drastically need programs to promote committed relationships and cooperation. As a nation, we have developed the phenomenal technological and scientific advancements required to land on the moon, cure heretofore incurable diseases, and to achieve numerous other ingenious feats.

Yet our greatest problems lie beyond our ability to master the physical world by way of technological advancements. Our greatest dilemmas relate to the human spirit, individual motivation, and our ability to get along with others while we each pursue the improvement of our own individual lot in life.

The pages of this book highlight the ways in which co-curricular school activities enhance the classroom learning experience of students as well as their ability to cooperatively work with others. The message of *The Importance of School Sports in American Education and Socialization* clarifies the need for high quality school sports and other co-curricular programs directed by professionally trained educators. This is a message of hope and empowerment for our youth and our nation.

November 19, 1993
Notre Dame, Indiana   Theodore M. Hesburgh, C. S. C.

Preface

There is no shortage today of the dismal accounts of our educational system, particularly in public schools. Numerous books and articles have been published alerting us to the high percentage of negative standardized test results, employers' reports of incompetent literacy skills among employees who graduated from high school as well as college. Daily newspaper accounts report depressing stories of the dangerous environments existing on many school campuses across the nation due to youth gangs and great numbers of students who carry weapons to school. Editorial pages frequently present articles and letters which portray the pessimistic outlook prevalent among so many people in America today regarding American public education. Add to this negative picture the growing number of concerns of increasing cultural pluralism in the U.S., and one can find plenty of reasons to feel pessimistic about both our nation's system of education and future in general.

But then, I recently observed a stage play put on by a school dramatics group in which students from different cultural backgrounds collaborated to successfully produce. And, I watched a culturally diverse high school football team of youth work, sweat, strive, make mistakes, overcome some of those mistakes, endure the repercussions of mistakes made and not corrected, support one another and generally struggle for individual and team success. I also recently read the names of the editorial staff and contributing writers of a school newspaper which reflected different cultural backgrounds.

In each of these instances, I felt a sense of optimism because of the positive interactions and collaborations I observed. I am optimistic because of the mutual care I see - not devoid of internal conflicts and struggles, but in spite of these obstacles - mutual endeavors to achieve individual and group improvement. My optimism is strengthened when I observe the people who come to see the performances of these school groups. And it all takes place without those involved in these pursuits being forced to participate; all the participants are involved voluntarily!

Ironically and unfortunately, these educational activities in which students voluntarily participate are, at best, deemphasized and are usually disregarded altogether in serious conversations about education. Variously referred to as co-curricular or extracurricular programs, these learning activities most frequently take place before or after the hours in which school classroom hours activities are conducted. *The Importance of School Sports in American Education and Socialization* is about this second category of learning activities.

No activity is more important to the continuance and welfare of our nation than the education of our young in the core curriculum subject matter including math, physical and social sciences, and literary arts. In addition, classroom courses in music, dramatics and art are very important for the understanding of human cultural and creative capacities. Learning these and other subjects taught in the classroom are fundamental to help youth develop knowledge about themselves, their local, national, and world communities and to learn skills that will help prepare them for post school work and to contribute to the improvement of our society and world.

In light of the importance of the core curriculum in American education, though, the value of learning experiences in co-curricular activities have been unwisely overlooked or underrated in their importance. Education should be just as much about learning to cooperate with others for the benefit of community interests as we each pursue our own individual interests. As discussed at length in chapter 3, more has been accomplished through collaboration than competition. Yet competition is a fundamental principle of our free enterprise economic system and our republican political system. Youth need to learn and practice both cooperation and fairly conducted competition as much as they need to be educated in the subjects of the core curriculum.

I am aware of the many benefits I gained from my participation in co-curricular activities: bonding with others, identifying and pursuing achievement of goals, learning the meaning of commitment to those goals and to something greater than myself: the team and the honor of the school community. I learned the value of persistence in the face of adversity and defeat, the importance of give-and-take with others, the importance of self-discipline, and that the possibilities for successful human achievement are dramatically increased when individuals join in dedicated spirit with others in a positive and mutually caring effort. Testimonies of similar worthwhile experiences gained from participation in co-curricular programs have been made by many others.

Considering these observations of positive efforts and interactions among youth, however, several questions regarding the true significance of co-curricular programs occurred to me. Are these voluntary school activities just youthful amusements to occupy students' after-class time to keep them out of trouble? Are these activities really extra or non-essential since they are variously referred to as extracurricular activities? Or, do they have any real educational value? Or, might these programs provide important, even essential educational benefits to students? Is it possible that co-curricular programs benefit our nation as well as, if differently, as core curricular educational programs?

This book attempts to answer these and other questions regarding the critical benefits of these programs to our youth and nation.

During the writing of this work, I have been blessed to receive the reactions of many very special people. A few are associated with my beloved alma mater, the University of Notre Dame. The Executive Director of Alumni of Notre Dame, Chuck Lennon, who was also one of my educational consultants, was very gracious and helpful in availing his time and consideration to this project.

Ara Parseghian, my college football coach at Notre Dame, was very encouraging and generous with his time. Ara was as much an educator as he was an athletic coach and is a credit to educators in general.

A very special thank you to Father Theodore Hesburgh, C.S.C., Notre Dame's President Emeritus, who served as the University's President for 35 years. In addition to providing outstanding leadership during that time, Father Ted's esteemed scholarship is evidenced by the 111 honorary degrees he has received from as many institutions of higher learning in the United States and around the world. Also during this busy 35 year period, he served for 15 years as a member and a chairman of the Civil Rights Commission. Throughout all his academic career and leadership, he maintained one stance regarding co-curricular programs including sports: academics are to be always first in priority! If anyone in America is an inspiration for and role model of high quality education in our country, Father Ted is. And I greatly appreciate his belief in the importance of school co-curricular programs and his support of my work.

Sincere thanks also go to Dr. Nel Noddings, Dean of Stanford University's School of Education. In addition to her encouragement of my work, I appreciate the important insights she shared with me from her many years as an educator and parent of ten children.

I thank John W. Gardner for his kind permission to draw on his significant writings regarding the development and regeneration of community. His many years of scholarship and public service as Secretary of Health, Education and Welfare and several other high level positions of leadership have provided him with significant experience and insights about fundamental aspects of any civilization, including communication and community. I greatly appreciate the contribution of his ideas to this work.

An important part of the research for this book was consulting with professionals from the fields of education, social work, and law enforcement who regularly deal with youth and youth-related social problems. Although I met with each of them for the first time during respective individual interviews, I was impressed by the personal courtesy, dedication, and extensive experience of these professionals. Except for Tracy Robinson who had 5 years of experience in his position at the time of our interview, the consultants averaged 20-30 years each in their professional areas.

While all responsibility for this work is mine, I owe much appreciation to this group for sharing with me their observations. I did not know the consultants' personal experiences and opinions about education in general or co-curricular school programs in particular prior to the informational interview with each person. However, it was very interesting to note that all of them claim that co-curricular school programs provide very important experiences in the education and socialization of youth in our nation. For the sake of brevity, I refer to the consensus of their observations at different points within the text. For the purpose of reference, therefore, following is a descriptive list of consultants:

Don Bell, M.A., Principal, Leland High School, San Jose, CA
Phil Corkill, Ed.D., Associate Superintendent, Flowing Wells School
    District, Tucson, AZ
Barbara Dawson, Ph.D., Principal, Piedmont Hills High School,
    San Jose, CA
John Fernandez, Ph.D., Director of the Empowerment of Hispanic
    Students and Their Families Program, East Side Unified High
    School District, San Jose, CA
Chuck Gary, M.A., Principal, Milpitas High School, Milpitas, CA
Jim Kelley, Ph.D., Education District Sales Manager,
    Apple Computer, Inc., Nashville, TN and former school
    principal and administrative assistant for the State of Tennessee

Department of Education
Chuck Lennon, M.A., Unified School District Board Member, South
Bend, IN
Monica Lodge, M.A., Athletic Director, Los Altos High
School, Los Altos, CA
Nel Noddings, Ph.D., Associate Dean, School of Education, Stanford
University, Stanford, CA
Lieutenant Dan Ortega, Commander of Violent Crimes Unit, Police
Department, San Jose, CA
Ben Parks, M.A., Head Wrestling Coach, Menlo-Atherton High
School, Menlo Park, CA
Roberto Perez, Ph.D., Vice Principal, Willow Glen High School, San
Jose, CA
Tracy Robinson, Coordinator of the Gang Enforcement Unit of the
Office of the City Attorney, Los Angeles, CA
Bob Shannon, M.A., Head Football Coach and Teacher, East St. Louis
High School, East St. Louis, IL
Eddie Subega, M.S., Program Manager, Alum Rock Counseling
Center Crisis Intervention Program for Youth, San Jose, CA
Eddie Titus, Probation Officer, Santa Clara County, CA
Gil Villagran, M.S., Project Coordinator Nuestra Casa Youth
Leadership Project, Santa Clara County, CA
Fred Villasenor, Executive Director, Community Coordinated Child
Development Center, San Jose, CA

Particular thanks go to those consultants who also provided critical commentary after reading the manuscript: Drs. Barbara Dawson, Roberto Perez, Phil Corkill, Jim Kelley, and Coach Ben Parks. And a very special thanks to Don Bell for his extensive time and effort in reviewing the manuscript. The consistent high ranking of student achievements at Leland High School reflects his outstanding leadership and high personal standards for excellence.

I also thank another outstanding educator, Sal Cesario, Principal at Pioneer High School in San Jose, for his very helpful support of this project.

For their additional critical reviews of the manuscript, thanks very much to Ian Cribbs, Mark Brown, Terry Daily, Bob Arboit, and Trish Siddens, a very special teacher. Much appreciation also goes to Bob Arboit for all his friendship and support since he gave me my first teaching and coaching job 20 years ago. Thanks also to authors Jim Thompson, Karl Laucher, and Mike Celizic for helpful advice.

Max Messmer was another valued reviewer and good friend whose perspectives and support are always appreciated.

The generosity of Dr. Art Ting, orthopedic surgeon for the San Jose professional hockey team is appreciated more than I can express here.

Over the years, several people have been valuable friends and sources of encouragement in the development of ideas presented in this work. Many thanks to John Thurau, Steve Stubbs, Larry Rouse, Ted Mackin, Steve Caria, and Tom Barnes for being strong sources of encouragement in my work on this project. Gary Beckman has been as good a friend and inspiration as one can hope for; many thanks to him, also.

I am indebted to Mitch Bostian, an outstanding English teacher and high school wrestling coach, for his superb editing of the manuscript. Also, for providing excellent assistance in the final preparation of this work, I am very grateful to Stan Oparowski of Almaden Press in San Jose, CA.

Sincere appreciation for encouragement and research suggestions or information goes to Drs. Jay Chambers and Bob Rossi of the American Institute of Research, Greg Payne of San Jose State University, Martha Ewing of Michigan State University, Pat McSwegin and Cindy Pemberton of the University of Missouri at Kansas City, Paul Warren, Dean of the University of San Francisco School of Education, Jeff Owings and Vance Grant of the U.S. Department of Education, James Fulton of the California Department of Education, Betty Hennessy, Consultant for the Los Angeles County Office of Education, and Helen Upton of the National Federation of High School Associations. Thanks also for information related to California Department of Corrections costs to James Tilton, Deputy Director of the Administrative Services Division of that agency.

Ideas expressed are really an extension and continuation of untold numbers of my predecessors: student-participants, teachers, coaches, mentors, and parents from early originators of school co-curricular activities to those who currently continue to make these valuable experiences for our youth possible. I was strongly influenced by the accumulated experiences of my teachers, coaches, mentors and close friends. Their encouragement and support both in my sports or other activities was helpful to my own personal and interpersonal development both in and out of the classroom. I wish space would allow mention of all those I would like to acknowledge. However, I will have to satisfy myself in recognizing by name the following individuals among the many more wonderful people who have made a positive difference in my life enroute to completing this work.

Particular thanks and appreciation to Gene Knutson, University of Michigan All-American and former Green Bay Packer who was a very positive role model as a teacher and athletic coach for me as a high school student and afterwards. Thanks also to Bucky Haag and Bob Otolski, teachers and athletic coaches during my high school years.

Affection and appreciation to life-long friends and teammates, Mike Earley and John Bognar. Also, appreciation goes to Susie Ball Laurie and Kathy Miller Will. Their caring friendship always meant so much during the vicissitudes of youthful days.

For their strong positive influence during my undergraduate college days, much gratitude to sociology professor Bob Vasoli, a demanding teacher under whose direction I struggled and gained beyond measure, and to Fathers Tom Brennan (deceased), B.H. Lange (deceased), and James Burtchaell, C.S.C. I am also grateful to my primary graduate school professors for their valuable guidance: Steve Zlutnick, Ken Blaker, Mary Ann Wakefield, and Barry Hayes.

Belated appreciation goes to college teammates who exemplify the best in student-athletes as well as friendship during our college years and since: Nick Eddy, Lou Fournier, George Goeddeke, Danny Gibbs (deceased), Kevin Hardy, John Horney, John Lium, Jim Lynch, Joe Marsico, Paul Seiler, Dick Swatland, and Tim Wengierski.

Jack Snow was a special All-American football player at Notre Dame and an All-Pro with the Los Angeles Rams; he was just as much an all-star friend and I thank him very much for being like an older brother from whom I took inspiration during my early college years.

Anyone who has served in the United States Marine Corps knows that team work and commitment that are so important in school co-curricular activities are epitomized in the Marines. Much appreciation to all the Marines with whom I served following my graduation from college and in particular to: Kim Butts, Art Bausch, John Markel, Norm Hapke, Jon Hass, Tom Hribar, Don Malone, Lee Kinney, and Jon Rider.

During seven years of graduate school, I worked in athletic fund-raising for the Bronco Bench Foundation which strongly supports the intercollegiate athletic program at Santa Clara University. I have much appreciation of the many wonderful people for and with whom I worked. These are people who believe in and support high school co-curricular activities as much as or more than college programs. Again, there are too many to acknowledge each by name. So I must satisfy myself by expressing particular appreciation to the following individuals who provided extraordinary support to my work in time and effort: Bill Antonioli, John and Joe Albanese, Sal Campisi, Barbara Hansen, Jack Healey, Clyde LeBaron, Tom Narey, Bud Ogden, Rick Ravizza, Phil Sanfilippo, Sal Sanfilippo (deceased), Lester and Nick Tikvica, Larry Schott, Frank Fiscalini, Al Wolff, Fr. Lou Bannon, Mike Fox, Nick Livak, Paul Neilan, Vic Giacalone, Ray Henningsen, Bill Crowley, Don Callejon, Ken Allen and Tom Zipse.

During the years I was an athletic coach, I was fortunate to get to know many fine young student-athletes; of special mention are: Mark Arvay, Janet Benton, Tom Bordenave, Mark Bruening, Mike Cummins, John Hurley, Gary Gardner, Greg Mooney, Dennis McClenahan, and Mary Nulk.

In particular, much affection and appreciation to four of these former student-athletes and friends who are like family and who have had a very positive influence on my life: Dave Cardona, Dr. Richard Lopez, Steve Mata, and Bobby Serrano.

One of my best friends who epitomized good character and care for others prior to his untimely death in 1985 was Pat Malley, head football coach and athletic director at Santa Clara University for 28 years. The message of this work greatly reflects the wonderful inspiration he gave to so many, students - athletes and non-athletes alike.

Butch Hamann, Jack Going, Steve Schott, Sam Gerardi, and Kevin Eagleson exemplify the best in people and friends. My appreciation to them for their extensive support in time and effort to my work as well as their loyal friendship over the past 17 years.

Jerry Kerr is one of the best people and friends ever. He has done more for Santa Clara University, countless others, and me than can adequately be repaid him. For the sake of acknowledgment now, much affection and appreciation to him and his wife, Jean, will have to do.

Much love and appreciation to the memory of my deceased parents, Harry and Jane Jeziorski. Finally, the greatest burden of all the hours I have spent in researching and writing this work has been incurred by my family. My greatest love and appreciation to my son, Jeff, my daughter, Jenny and my wife, Jane.

Please note that chapter 6, in the first printing of this text, due to incomplete information, misrepresented the PAC's statistics. This issue updates this information.

Chapter 1

The Best & Worst of Times For American Youth

> It was the best of times, it was the worst of times, it was the age of
> wisdom, it was the age of foolishness, it was the epoch of belief, it was
> the epoch of incredulity, it was the season of darkness, it was the spring
> of hope, it was the winter of despair, we had everything before us, we
> had nothing before us...

Although written in 1859, these words with which Charles Dickens
began his classic story, *A Tale of Two Cities*, sadly reflect the condition of
present-day American social problems, particularly as they apply to our
youth. On the one hand, our civilization can claim the greatest technological advancements and accumulation of knowledge ever. We have
achieved the greatest standard of living in history. Yet we are plagued by
certain conditions which have never been worse regarding other aspects
of our culture. We have social ills that our great technological and scientific advancements have fallen short of resolving. And, with the exception of the family unit, no American institution has been hit worse by the
onslaught of social disorders than our schools.

To clarify the dramatic progression of social problems in our schools,
social and political analyst George Will provides us a backdrop for comparison of the drastic change in concerns of public school students over
the past forty years. In his book, *Suddenly*, Will (1990) describes two
surveys reflecting problems common to America's public schools, the
first one taken in the 1940's and the second in the 1980's. The 1940's
survey listed the following concerns: talking, chewing gum, making noise,
getting out of turn in line, not putting paper in wastebaskets, running in
the halls, and wearing improper clothes. The 80's survey listed the following as the top problems: drug and alcohol abuse, teenage pregnancy,
suicide, rape, robbery, assault (35).

There's nothing subtle about the contrasting issues reflected in these
two surveys. Violence in our nation is at an all-time high. Sadly, the segment of our society with the highest incidence of crime and violence as

well as the highest incidence of suicide is that of adolescents between the ages of 15 and 19. The rate of suicides among this population has increased 300% since 1950. In fact, suicide ranks as the second leading cause of death among all teenagers. These statistics have been corroborated by the results of a recent Stanford University study by economics researchers Victor Fuchs and Diane Reklis (Moore, 1992). Drug use and abuse continues to increase among teens each year as the average age of initial use by youth is now 13 years old; and 33% of American high school seniors average intoxication at least once each week. Among black males, the situation is even worse as 25% of this population are in prison or under court supervision (Coats, 1991).

The stability of home life for many young people continues to be weakened because of an increasingly high divorce rate and increasing number of births to unwed teens, many of whom are often addicted to drugs. In fact, approximately 500,000 such births occur annually in the United States. The continued high incidence of divorce results in a growing percentage of our nation's youth living in homes with only one natural parent. The National Commission on Children reported on June 24, 1991 that many of our nation's youth are living in circumstances that will adversely affect their chances for well-adjusted and productive adulthood (Zaldivar & Spears, 1992). The Commission also alerts us to the fact that

> Investing in children is no longer a luxury, but a national imperative.... America's future as a democratic nation, a world leader and an economic power will depend as much on youngsters who are ill educated, alienated or poor as on those who are more advantaged (McFeaters, 1991).

The national picture of our youth problems is a grim one. But we can take heart; we can improve the picture by following the Commission's warning voice. If we increase educational and other constructive youth programs, we can stem the progressive rise in the deplorable conditions of youth in this country, in much the same way that once-failing individual and group health conditions have improved.

A unique parallel exists between the health of a society and the health of an individual, a parallel with implications for educational programs in our schools. Over the past two decades, studies in the health sciences have provided valuable information about methods that can be used to prevent illnesses and promote good individual health. Until the relatively recent implementation of disease prevention programs such as stress management techniques, improved dietary habits, and regular exercise, traditional attitudes regarding health were along the lines of, "If it ain't broke, don't fix it." Spiraling medical costs, however, forced Americans to consider alternative approaches to reverse the negative health trend. Fortunately, where preventive maintenance and health medicine programs have been implemented in America, health records have improved and costs have decreased.

Unfortunately, we are seeing the antithesis of this progress develop in the socialization (i.e., the process by which a culture introduces and teaches its norms and mores to its youth) and educational experience of a large and ever-increasing segment of our nation's youth. Continued funding cuts in educational classroom and co-curricular programs contribute to the further erosion of youth, our most valuable resource for the future. As we decrease quality opportunities for youth participation in required classroom activities, even more voluntary co-curricular programs, including sports, school newspaper, dance, debate and drama, band and choral groups, have been eliminated from schools. Among the many negative results of such program cuts are five particularly harmful developments among youth: (a) deviant behavior; (b) increased susceptibility to negative influences; (c) decreased opportunities to experience the democratic principles which are the basis of our Constitution; (d) lost educational experiences; and (e) lost time and expense to society in law enforcement activities.

First Task of Education:
Student Attendance & Involvement

In both education and the retail industry, a sale must be made to achieve desirable results. In a retail business, the sale involves an exchange of the customer's money for some type of merchandise (product or service). In education, the sale is made when a student is motivated to learn (the student's "money" being his effort to learn) the school's educational merchandise (the curriculum information). In both cases, the sale (customer exchanges money for goods, a student tries to learn) takes place only after the prospective buyer (customer in a store, student in a school) is sufficiently motivated to do so.

In the retail industry, the first and most important task in selling a store's products is to get people into the store. Otherwise, any other aspect of making a sale and a profit is pointless. Prospective buyers can't buy until they come into the store. Strange as it may initially seem, this old commercial marketing slogan metaphorically applies to our contemporary problems in the education and socialization of our nation's youth: the first task in educating youth is to get them into our schools. While this is perhaps the most crucial concern in retail sales, legal requirements for school attendance have inadvertently eliminated such a concern in our educational system.

Every day, throughout the school year, American youth convene at our schools...by mandate. Not only are these regular conventions required by law, they are also part of daily life expectations in our country. But before we can hope that young people will learn once they arrive at our schools, they must first stay there and actively participate in the educational process.

It is true that a relatively small but growing number (considerably larger number in inner city schools) of our school age children cut school and many put forth little or no effort to learn. Others disrupt classroom learning efforts with misbehavior. Such uncooperative behaviors can be traced to one or more of a myriad of problems. Limited or no parental support and emotional problems due to continued breakup of the American family are just two examples.

However, in spite of all the problems which negatively affect the education and socialization of our youth today, we still have one major advantage over our metaphorical retail store motto: THE VAST MAJORITY OF YOUTH DO SHOW UP! In logic similar to that of the old retail marketing adage, every day we get the prospective buyers (students) into the stores (schools)! But do our youthful prospective "buyers" of intellectual, physical, and social learning experiences want to stay after they arrive? Do they wish to seriously consider the important value of these educational offerings? For increasing numbers of American youth, the answers to these questions would be negative as indicated by unfavorable academic performance scores, undesirable classroom behavior, increased student violence at schools, and increasing drop-out rates. Are means available to motivate these youth to actively participate in school and "buy" the offerings of our schools? According to testimony offered by the educational consultants for this book and other indicators, the answer is YES!

Positive Correlation of Co-curricular Participation and School Performance

Unfortunately, we have witnessed over the past quarter century an erosion of important programs which favorably influence youth to stay in school and "buy" the offerings of our educational system: co-curricular (also referred to as "extracurricular") activities. These voluntary activities provide myriad challenges and opportunities for youth to develop intrapersonal qualities of commitment and determination, as well as interpersonal skills of cooperation so greatly needed in our democratic society. Participation in co-curricular programs integrates youth from diverse backgrounds and promotes democratic principles of our nation, including individual rights, freedoms, equality, protection of the common good.

These co-curricular activities also facilitate learning experiences that involve facing difficult individual and group challenges, learning to persevere and keep trying during difficult times, learning to overcome defeats, learning to strive for self-improvement yet sacrifice self-interests when needed, and learning to cooperate with teammates even when tensions develop between participants. While many youth today seek security and affiliation in gang involvements, co-curricular programs offer alternative constructive ways for youth to experience hope and develop mutually supportive relationships with peers and mentors.

In America, approximately 1 million or 12% of our students drop out of school each year! It is no small statement that we need educational programs which encourage youth to remain in school. School sports and other co-curricular programs often act as antidotes for dropping out of school. They motivate many students to stay in school, and they can be used to prompt students to improve interest and efforts in studying classroom subjects.

Across the board, the educational consultants described in the Preface as well as other educators noted in this book, testify that co-curricular participants generally earn higher grades, behave better in the classroom, and drop out of school less than non-participants. Reasons offered by these administrators and teachers for the better average performance of co-curricular participants included: the discipline and work ethic exercised in co-curricular activities carry over into the classroom; the mentors of participants evoke positive behaviors that carry over; participants may carry structure of their co-curricular activities into their core curriculum classes; in order to participate in co-curricular activities students have to maintain a 2.0 grade point average; and they have a sense of purpose and being a part of something bigger than themselves as a member of a team that non-participants may not have.

Results from a 1985 national survey, sponsored by the National Federation of State High School Associations, funded by the Lilly Endowment, and conducted by Indiana University, strongly complement these testimonies. Findings revealed that 95% of all principals surveyed believe that co-curricular programs facilitate valuable learning experiences not generally available in the classroom; equally significant, 99% said that co-curricular activities promote citizenship.

These observations tended to be corroborated by findings of studies based on data gathered by the U.S. Department of Education's National Center for Education Statistics. One study was presented in a 1986 report by the National Center with the heading, "Extracurricular Activity Participants Outperform Other Students" (U.S. Department of Education National Center for Statistics Bulletin, 1986). Findings were drawn from the data base of the Center's longitudinal study, "High School & Beyond." Subjects were randomly selected from a highly stratified probability sample which represented America's high school sophomore population of approximately 3.8 million in 1980, the base year of the study. In that year, data were gathered on approximately 28,000 10th graders as follows: amount of time spent on homework was determined from subject self-report questionnaires; number of course credits earned and grade point averages for each subject were identified on school transcripts and other information completed by school officials; and subjects' standardized test scores on vocabulary, reading, and math.

In 1982, data were gathered on follow-up administrations of the same measures and information sources from the base year for a subsample of 16,200 (when subjects had advanced to high school seniors from the larger 1980 participant sample) and compared for differences. Findings indicated that, compared to non-participants, co-curricular participants put more time into completing homework, had higher scores on the standardized tests, and were much less likely to have a 2.0 or less g.p.a. In addition, those who earned more course credits tended to be more involved in co-curricular programs.

Focusing specifically on high school sports participants, the Women's Sports Foundation sponsored another study using subjects from the National Center's 1980 base year longitudinal data, and 3 follow-up assessments of the same information for a subsample of 12,000 in 1982, 1984, and 1986. Findings from those analyses were broken down into 6 different subgroups consisting of females and males for each of 3 racial/ethnic backgrounds: Black, Hispanic, and White student-subjects. As the Women's Sports Foundation points out in its report (1989), this study is the first to be conducted by a national sports governing body on the effects of high school sports that considers ethnic and racial participation.

Results of the analyses generally indicated favorable effects of sports participation on motivation to earn higher grades. For Hispanic and White females and White men, school sports participation had a significant positive correlation with higher grades. While statistical differences for Hispanic males and Black females and males were not significant, the trends toward higher grade levels favored these 3 groups compared to non-sports participants. The National Federation of State High School Associations reports similar positive findings regarding higher grade point average of co-curricular participants over those of non-participants as found in studies conducted by four state high school activity associations: the Minnesota State High School League, the Iowa High School Athletic Association, and the Kansas State and North Dakota High School Activities Associations.

Similar to the above analyses conducted by the U.S. DepartmentEducation's National Center for Educational Statistics, the Women's Sports Foundation study revealed significantly higher scores on the standardized achievement tests in vocabulary, reading and mathematics for school sports participants when compared to non-participants of all 6 subgroups.

Regarding drop-outs, trends in the Womens' Sports Foundation's findings for several of the subgroups agreed with the educational consultants' observations. Unfortunately, for subgroups dominated by those living in urban areas, there was no difference in drop-out rates indicated for school sports participants when compared to non-participants. The authors of the report speculated that this latter finding could very well be associated with negative effects of poverty, crime, broken families, and other pervasive social ills as predominant in large American cities today. Such a connection appears to be a very valid consideration since school sports - as positive an influence as they might generally present - are only one among many influences which impinge upon youth living in such dire circumstances.

In a longitudinal study initiated in 1988, the National Center for Education Statistics intends to examine changes over time in student subjects, with the intent of identifying the effects of various aspects of the educational system and other potential influences on student behavior and school performance. Subjects were randomly selected from a highly stratified probability sample of 24,599 eighth graders from 1,052 American public and private schools. Initial data were collected in the base year of 1988 via individual questionnaires completed by student subjects, their parents and teachers. The subjects also completed standardized cognitive tests in math, science, reading, and social studies. To compare student progress over time, follow-up data were collected via similar instruments two years later in 1990, when the subjects were to be in their sophomore year of high school. On the individual questionnaire, question number 66F asks if the student-respondent attended school because he or she was on a team. Over 45% of the 24,599 respondents indicated that they, in fact, attended school because they were on a team (National Center for Education Statistics, 1992).

Optimistic findings of lowered drop-out rates for co-curricular participants were further reflected in a Kansas State High School Association report, which established that in a one year period, 96% of drop-outs in Kansas were non-participants. In a separate study, the National Federation of High School Associations reported similar findings.

More studies are needed to further examine the correlation of school sports and other co-curricular programs to the incidence of drop-outs. However, the 45% affirmative reply by respondents to question 66F supports the testimony of our educational consultants. Such a reply makes sense given the combination of widespread broken families and adolescents' great need to seek affiliation and security; both of which are commonly found on a sports team...and, unfortunately, in gang involvements.

Always a Price to Pay, Now or Later:
Which Will We Pay?

Widespread cuts in school budgets across America have weakened, and are increasingly eliminating, these voluntary educational programs which provide hope and direction for hundreds of thousands of youth. Yet opportunities to satisfy their needs for attention, affiliation, and hope proliferate via drugs and gang involvements. These socially destructive activities have dramatically increased in frequency as constructive co-curricular programs have been cut back or eliminated, even though they are needed more than ever. In weakening such programs, we have lost valuable means of inducing young people to go to school and become proactively involved in the classroom as well. By decreasing the quality and number of co-curricular school activities, we also forfeit programs which dissuade youth from gang involvements and deviant behavior. The destructive repercussions that eventually result are often naively ignored or not expected to occur by those responsible for the cuts. A typical example of these circumstances took place in New York City in 1991.

Early that year, the New York City Board of Education cut the junior varsity teams from the school sports programs in the boroughs of Brooklyn and Queens. At first glance, such a move might appear to be warranted because of the Board's need to reduce its budget. One might assume that, regrettable as this event is, it is merely a matter of eliminating an opportunity for several hundred prospective student-athletes to play sports. Not that big of a deal.

However, New York State Senator Alton R. Waldon, Jr., has cause to disagree strongly, as he clearly describes the greater long-term negative effects of such an action in the following letter to the Editor of the New York Times. As a former law enforcement officer with considerable first-hand experience dealing with youth problems, his observations offer valuable insight.

To the Editor:

As a New York State Senator with an extensive background in law enforcement, I have seen how well preventive measures can work in the battle against drugs and crime.

Despite the money crunch that threatens many New York City and state programs, we must spare after-school athletics. We cannot overlook their worth. For the kid who lacks self-confidence, positive role models or parental guidance, belonging to a team can be a way to steer clear of drug use and other harmful activities that may lead straight into the criminal justice system.

I am calling for restoration of the junior varsity athletic programs in Brooklyn and Queens, which the city's Board of Education recently eliminated to save money. This action has robbed 7,000 high school students of a way to say no to the dangerous pressures of the street.

But Mayor David N. Dinkins and other city leaders can restore the athletic programs with money that will become available under the Safe Streets, Safe City Act. This recently enacted state law provides $60

million a year for youth education and crime prevention for children at
risk.

    The junior varsity athletic programs cost only $2 million a year,
and without them, many children are much more at risk than they were
before. Doesn't it make more sense to pay $2 million now for extracur-
ricular athletic pro grams that help keep our kids out of trouble in stead
of millions in social service and criminal justice costs later?

    For most of these kids, it's not a question of later. It's now or never
(Waldon, 1991).

Senator Waldon's appeal to the Board of Education echoes the popular television advertisement of 20 years ago for Fram automobile oil fil-
ters, in which the mechanic tells the owner of a car in need of an oil
change: "It's up to you, sir. You can pay me now or pay me later." Of
course, it was explained in the commercial that buying the new oil filter
"now," at $15, would prevent damage to the engine and cost a very small
fraction of the later cost of an engine repair. In terms of cost, this advertisement is a somewhat easily understood metaphor regarding the cost of
preventing disease among people, whether on an individual physical and
mental health basis or in terms of social conditions including youth-related problems of today.

    The mounting costs of housing inmates of our federal, state, county
and municipal penal institutions help us to appreciate the Fram oil filter
metaphor. It costs over $20,750 a year to house a prisoner in California.
With 117,300 California state prison inmates at the end of 1993, the total
cost just for the upkeep of inmates in the California state prisons was
over $2.43 billion. When we consider that this cost excludes all other
types of costs to the law enforcement, justice, and penal systems, $2.44
billion is only part of the much larger price tag we pay. As an example, it
costs California taxpayers over $170 million for the supervision of over
85 thousands parolees during 1993. The financial loss to the citizens of
California includes millions of dollars more for all other types of costs to
the law enforcement, justice systems under city and county jurisdiction.

    However, within the context of a preventive model regarding social
and legal problems, the same $20,750 that pays for a criminal's housing
will fund a high school football program involving approximately 55
student-participants. Or, it will pay for the majority of other co-curricular
programs for girls and boys, including about 35 students for involved in
fall, winter, and spring sports. Clearly, we do pay a much higher price

later, for our resulting social cancers, when we avoid investing in constructive educational youth programs. The Fram oil filter advertisement provides a valuable message for us: funding programs such as co-curricular school activities is a much less costly way of deterring destructive/self-defeating behaviors in lieu of later more costly measures of state and local law enforcement and corrections departments.

Gangs:
Alternative Activities for Affiliation and Security

The current scenario has all the components for a national tragedy. As the break-up of the family continues to plague America, young people increasingly seek security and affiliation that all too often are readily available in gangs. Young people need to affiliate with others their age, feel a part of a group, and feel appreciated for whom they are, even as they struggle to know themselves. In fact, much of how they see themselves comes from those with whom they associate. Students who are denied opportunities for constructive involvements and camaraderie with peers will surely fulfill these needs elsewhere...as we are seeing! Unfortunately, the "elsewhere" is often gang activities.

The disconcerting situation regarding youth gangs in our society is clarified by Tracy Robinson, Coordinator of the Gang Enforcement Unit of the Los Angeles City Attorney's Office. Tracy has considerable experience with gang members and their parents. As part of the City Attorney's "Parenting Program," he meets with parents of youth who are referred by law enforcement officials to his office as being "at-risk" for gang involvement and deviant behaviors. He also visits with gang members on the streets of Los Angeles and speaks at various city junior high and senior high schools, churches and other community groups regarding retardation of youth and gang problems. His ongoing experiences with youth involved in gang activities give much validity to his testifying to the viability of co-curricular programs. According to Robinson:

> It doesn't just happen that kids simply join any gang. They are recruited. The reigning gang in a neighborhood identifies the young children in that "hood" as members-to-be of that gang. That assumption is strongly conveyed to children and acts as a form of psychological pressure for the youth to join eventually.

In South Central Los Angeles, where the 1992 riots resulted in 62 deaths, multiple injuries, and fires that destroyed millions of dollars worth of property, youth have few alternatives to gang activities. Robinson further explains:

> Apart from the material attractions of girls, money, clothing, and sometimes shelter, gangs provide security friendship, love, support and kindness. You will see the same outpouring of love and emotional support among members of a gang at the funeral of a fellow member as you find among the friends and family of anyone else's funeral. It is a lot like what you often see displayed by members of a sports team. Such emotional bonding is difficult to break once it is formed (Robinson, 1992).

Trust and Continuity: Essential to Youth

Another element which relates to youths' needs for security and emotional support, normally provided by an intact family and too often found only through gang membership, is trust and trusting relationships. Trust is the most basic element in any relationship. Without trust, there can be no viable and honest relationship. As they search for independence and struggle with self-identity and peer pressure, adolescents need positive activities in which they can voluntarily participate to help them in their individual and interpersonal development. They need practical experiences in successfully interacting with others. They need adults who are interested in them such as coaches and mentors who are deeply involved with them, and who will guide and demonstrate care for them on a regular basis. One of their most important needs is continuity of purpose, people, place, and focus of learning or curriculum.

Dr. Nel Noddings, Associate Dean of Stanford University's School of Education, provides valuable observations regarding the significance of continuity in adult caring to the development of youth in *The Challenge to Care in Schools* (1992, 63-73). Having been an high school math teacher for 20 years before joining the Stanford faculty, in addition to raising a family of 10 children, her observations reach beyond mere rhetoric.

> ...we must understand that the school, like the family, is a multipurpose institution. It cannot concentrate only on academic goals any more than a family can restrict its responsibilities to, say, feeding and hous-

ing its children. The single-purpose view is not only morally mistaken, it is practically and technically wrong as well, because schools cannot accomplish their academic goals without attending to the fundamental needs for continuity and care...(63).

Dr. Noddings goes on to remind us that one of the main developmental needs of children is a sense of belonging. Therefore, providing children continuity of place and people in the majority of their educational experiences contributes to their perception of security and belonging. Of course, in her recommendation, she assumes that the physical surroundings of the school are made safe and that the teachers give strong evidence of their care for their students. She contends that the educational experience for children will be considerably more worthwhile if they remain in the same school and be allowed extended relationships with the same teachers for three or more years. Such extended relationships between students and the same faculty facilitate much greater potential for trust to be established.

The point is crystallized by former Secretary of Education, William J. Bennett:

> This, then, is the iron law of education: the "system" doesn't educate anyone. Individuals do. Yeats wrote, 'All the drop-scenes drop at once/Upon a hundred thousand stages,' and it is on those individual stages that the educational dream fails or succeeds...(Bennett, 1992, 78).

However, it is only when credibility can be established between the individual educator and individual students that education takes place; and credibility usually develops over an extended period of time, as noted by Nel Noddings.

As a teacher on the college, high school and junior high school levels of education, I have personally experienced how much the length of time in getting to know a student has affected my ability to establish rapport. The longer I have been able to interact with and get to know a student, the better chance I have had to be of assistance in his or her development. Afterall, the best educational experience occurs only after a strong sense of trust has been established over time. In addition to my own experience, I have observed this to be true for other teacher-student relationships.

The relationship established between teacher and student is far more influential in the degree to which most students learn any academic subject than the methods of instruction being used. This is particularly important in education today. Nel Noddings describes the situation well. As the homelife for an increasing number of youth is unsettled and, too often, very disruptive and even violent, continuity of place and relationships at school become increasingly important to the stability of millions of our youth.

School Sports: Opportunities for Continuity and Trust

School sports and other co-curricular programs provide excellent opportunities for continuity in the educational experiences of youth. In fact, over the twentieth century, these activities have generally provided more continuity in school relationships with faculty/mentors for American youth than those within the classroom. Traditionally, students who have participated in co-curricular activities continue in a developing relationship with the same coach or mentor for more than one year and often more than two or three.

In contrast, as an elementary student progresses to higher grade levels, he or she will have a different classroom teacher for each subsequent school year. Junior and senior high school students usually have a different teacher for each of their course subjects.

It is important to highlight here the significance in preparing professionals to be coaches and co-curricula mentors. Given the potential influence of mentors and coaches of co-curricular programs on youth, those appointed to these roles should be every bit as professionally educated and trained in principles of education and human behavior as classroom teachers.

This is not to say or imply in any way that classroom teachers do not regularly have profound positive effects on youth. Nor is it a comment that co-curricular mentors are inherently better at establishing trust. Again, it is as much a factor of time involved in the development of a trustworthy relationship, as emphasized by Dr. Nel Noddings. Co-curricular programs generally require coaches and mentors to spend considerably more time, both short and long term, with their student participants than classroom curricula activities.

A young person is much more likely to develop trust for a mentor with whom he or she has been involved over a continuous period of time.

Co-curricular programs generally provide for such an ongoing relationship. While classroom teacher-student relationships are interrupted every semester, or at least each new school year on average, continuity of purpose and relationships can be maintained in co-curricular programs as group/team and individual goals are defined, adjusted and pursued from one year to the next, always under the guidance of the same mentor.

Adolescents need and seek the trustworthy relationships that are available with peers and mentors in co-curricular programs on a voluntary basis. Yet financial support for these constructive programs has progressively decreased, resulting in the increased hiring of part-time, non-teacher/educator coaches and mentors as well as the cutting of some of these activities altogether. In the meantime, growing numbers of youth have pursued trusting relationships in gangs and other non-constructive affiliations.

Youth will attempt to achieve a sense of security and belonging in a negative, self-defeating way if they have no constructive options. And, as we will discuss further in the next chapter, youth will also pursue their own misguided behavior standards if they are not engaged in educational experiences under trusted mentors who will provide them with positive direction. In chapter 2, we will look more closely at this critical issue and at the value of co-curricular programs as practical means to instruct youth in constructive behavior principles. In particular, we will examine one of the most important principles that too often today is also one of the most ignored: self-restraint.

Chapter 2:

Behavior Standards, Self-Restraint & Implications for Democracy

We must adjust to changing times and still hold to unchanging principles.
- President Jimmy Carter, Inaugural Address, January 20, 1977

In addition to the continued increase in gang involvements, youth are increasingly turning to drugs and alcohol for a quick escape from the lack of direction and emotional pain they experience. They obviously do this for a feeling of euphoric escape, albeit a short-lived, and in the long run, a self-defeating one. But, as far as many youth living in impoverished conditions are concerned, who cares about what may come in the future? Today is what they have to cope with. Forget any discussion of the ethic calling for delayed gratification of pleasures and long term rewards following hard work and sacrifice as is regularly practiced in co-curricular activities. For disadvantaged youth today, it's the "get-it-while-you-can-and-as-fast-as-you-can" mentality, characteristic of desperate people, that motivates.

But, then, what else should we really expect from such a large percentage of our young people these days? In addition to the myriad of social problems discussed in chapter 1, U.S. teens watch 22.5 hours of television per week (Nielsen Media Research, 1992) which is approximately four times the amount of homework they complete in the same time period (National Center for Education Statistics, Appendix L, Questions 36A1 and 36A2, 1992). Meanwhile, youth are daily exposed to violence and free-and-easy, no-commitment sexual activity presented extensively in movies, even those rated PG-13, and in television programming (all for the sake of art, of course!).

While these behavior trends have contributed to the deteriorating conditions of our youth, they have even larger implications for the future of our country. A democracy can only be sustained to the degree citizens are ruled by popularly determined law and not by the whims of individuals or factions. Yet establishing socially beneficial behavior among the citizens of a nation is anchored in basic principles and individual disciplines that must be learned and developed at an early age. As anti-social behaviors increase among growing numbers of youth to satisfy their own immediate and insatiable, albeit self-defeating, desires, the social fabric of our nation becomes progressively frayed. Unless the fraying is brought under control by effective methods of socialization, including education, the fabric disintegrates altogether. Unless self-restraint is learned and exercised early in life, in the interests of oneself as well as those of others, it is much more difficult to develop in later years.

U.S. Senator Dan Coats of Indiana sharpens the point regarding the importance of individual self-discipline to the maintenance of freedom in society by quoting Edmund Burke, the eighteenth century English statesman who supported the American Revolution:

> Men are qualified for civil liberty in exact proportion to their disposition to put moral chains on their own appetites. Society cannot exist unless a controlling power upon will and appetite be placed somewhere, and the less of it there is within, the more there is without. It is ordained in the eternal constitution of things that men of intemperate minds cannot be free. Their passions forge their fetters (Coats, 1991, 19).

Youth problems have been increasing as programs which involve teamwork and self-discipline, such as school sports and other co-curricula, have been decreased or cut altogether. The strong concern expressed in the report of the National Commission on Children noted in chapter 1 should alert us to the importance of these programs in helping youth develop and regularly practice behavior standards that facilitate both individual and community freedoms.

Anomie, Relativism, and Mixed Messages

"Anomie" is a term sociologists use to refer to a breakdown of social rules among a segment of a larger population. When there is a decrease in or confusion about commonly held beliefs and customs of a society among a portion of that society's members, sociologists characterize the condition as anomie. Unfortunately, anomie is an appropriate term applied to the behavior of a growing number of the youth in our country. Such is the consequence of the decline in direction provided youth, a result of the fragmentation of the American family unit.

As the family unit in America has dramatically declined over the last 25-30 years, there has been an implicit, if not explicit, expectation that our schools could at least partially fill the void in providing youth with morals or values training. However, a dichotomy has evolved within the schools which has not only prevented them from getting the job done but has also added the proverbial "fuel to the fire" of growth in anomie.

Relativism

The decade of the '60's was a protracted period of controversy in which most figures and tenets of authority were continually being contested, on college campuses as well as city streets. Civil rights struggles and the Vietnam war set the stage for the continuous barrage of an antiestablishment mood. This mood of protest, questioning, and confrontation paved the way for the application, in many classrooms, of a non-confrontational approach to discussing moral principles. Learning about values and appropriate social behavior became identified with each student determining his or her own values and behavior standards.

In his book, *Why Johnny Can't Tell Right From Wrong*, Boston College Psychologist William K. Kilpatrick describes the key developments in the evolution of this dichotomy. Approximately 25 years ago, according to Dr. Kilpatrick, many schools across the U.S. began to adopt a new approach to teaching moral principles, an approach involving openness and choice on the part of students as a means to arrive at their own determinants for good and bad behavior. According to this approach, students would find deliberation of values more interesting and relevant if they were allowed to choose right and wrong for themselves. The times were right for this new "relativistic" approach, as traditional social mores were widely being questioned and increasingly assaulted as being wrong.

Adopted from the innovative (at the time) psychotherapeutic method introduced by Carl Rogers and reinforced by the works of Abraham Maslow, this approach to psychological counseling is referred to as "nondirective." Instead of acting as a "doctor who tells the patient what to do to get better," this method calls for the therapist to act as a "guide" for the person being counseled. In fact, in Rogerian nondirective therapy, the person being counseled is referred to as "client" rather than "patient." Instead of providing the person being counseled with advice as to what the right thing to do would be, Rogers' approach involves the counselor paraphrasing the counselee's voluntarily submitted statements.

According to Rogers, by being very open and supportive to the client and repeating (in other words) what the client says, the counselor reflects back the client's self-report and enables the client to better understand him or herself and the root of his or her problem. In this way, the counselor acts as a facilitator who assists the client in determining, on his or her own, what is most relevant to him or her enroute to understanding and resolving the problem. Ultimately, the counselor helps a client to clarify his or her life situation, and what he or she can do to improve it.

It was this non-confrontational approach to psychotherapy that was the basis for the new method of discussing moral issues or values in the classroom. Unsurprisingly, it was coined as "values clarification" or "moral reasoning." Following this approach, teachers present moral questions and hypothetical dilemmas to their classes. In turn, students decide for themselves the correct action to take in the hypothesized dilemma. Indeed, the values clarification approach seemed to work at the very beginning and was found to stimulate active discussion of moral issues. However, as indicated by the discouraging statistics regarding increased crime and self-destructive behavior among our youth, the values clarification approach to introducing and encouraging constructive and socially redeeming values has not been effective enough, if at all.

According to Dr. Kilpatrick, however, talking alone about hypothetical examples of moral conflicts is insufficient for development of values. He emphasizes that such a non-directive approach to classroom curriculum on morality or values

> ...assumes that such things as honesty, property rights, and human life are already valued by youngsters and, therefore, the only difficulty is to choose among these values when they conflict. That is, they assume a sort of natural goodness and integrity in the child, whereby he or she will always want to do the right thing. If there is a problem, it's only a problem of getting in touch with one's feelings or of learning to reason things out. The old idea that many of us suffer not from a defect in reasoning but a defect in character is not considered...The point is that [after a moral dilemma is presented to be reasoned out regarding, for instance, an issue related to stealing] the discussion whether or not to steal is only a dilemma for those who already think stealing is wrong (Kilpatrick, 1992, 86-87).

Boston University professor of ethics Edwin Delattre further clarifies Kilpatrick's position: "...No one can really have a dilemma or moral decision without already caring to be the kind of person who wants to discover the right thing to do and to have what it takes to do it (Kilpatrick, 8-87)." In other words, the person will or will not have a dilemma depending on the type of person he or she already is.

The personality of a youngster develops as he or she interacts with different environments and people in all his or her life circumstances. Kilpatrick points out that first-hand experiences in voluntarily dealing with others and facing personal responsibilities on regular basis with basic guidelines to conduct their behavior is when the "rubber can meet the road" in developing values among youth. Again, talking alone will not effect a development of values. The more constructive activities that a young person has in which he or she is confronted by moral conflicts similar to real life, the more likely he or she will be able to learn how to (effectively/appropriately) resolve such conflicts. The learning experience is particularly constructive and beneficial if a caring, professionally trained mentor is there to provide guidance when needed.

Mixed messages

We have already noted the dramatic breakdown of the family, the traditional source of moral teachings, and the deleterious effects this unfortunate situation has had on our nation's youth. If there is a primary factor in the development of anomie among our youth, it is the continuing spread of this social cancer.

Some of the most detrimental effects on youth resulting from a breakdown of the family are the repercussions prompted by parental mixed messages. In addition, mixed messages are widely presented by the various media in our country. No matter what their source, mixed messages are harmful to the development of values by the youth of our nation. Mixed messages act as communication "pollutants" to the "pool" of information to which youth are exposed and from which they construct their frames of reference in forming their own values. The balance of this chapter will focus on these contaminants of parent-child and media communications, as well as their impact on values development in youth.

For over a quarter of a century, substantial evidence has been found in studies of families and child rearing that, apart from outright abusive, antisocial, or even criminal behaviors modeled by parents, the most frequent parenting problems leading to behavior problems of youth result from mixed messages. The term "mixed messages" refers to any information explicitly or implicitly communicated to children by parents which contradicts, confuses, or otherwise conflicts with other parental messages or cues.

Mixed messages from parents have two basic forms. "Do as I say, not as I do," is an appropriate label for the first type, in which parents act in ways incongruent with what they tell their children to do or not to do (Walker & Sylvester, 1991, 15).

A second form of parental mixed message involves parents promising consequences for a child's performance or avoidance of a specific behavior. Then, when the child does what is or is not expected of him or her, the parent does not follow through with the consequences as promised. As a result, the child becomes confused and doubtful. In addition to causing confusion, both forms of mixed messages break down a child's trust regarding relationships, particularly with authority figures. Adults and children alike become confused from inconsistent communications in such relationships. Moreover, such inconsistencies in communication promote confusion and insecurity in a young person during the period he or she is still formulating his or her view of the world and his or her relation to it.

Compounding the problems of mixed messages from parents in our country are those broadcast by television programs, cinema arts and popular music. It is difficult to find a movie that is not rated "R" today. Blatant as well as subtle sexual activities with no commitments involved are regularly shown on T.V. and in movies. Given this, is there any wonder why irresponsible sexual activity, along with incidences of sexually transmitted diseases continually increases among teenagers? In fact, young people are engaging in sexual activity at earlier ages, as indicated by the Johns Hopkins University survey taken of rural schools in Maryland. It revealed that, by the time they were in the eighth grade, 61% of boys and 47% of girls had sexual intercourse (Gibbs, 60-61). But why not? Such deviant behavior is being regularly modeled and sanctioned in the most popular forms of public media!

On the other hand, this sexual freedom message is being confused by the contradictory media surveillance and coverage of extra-marital affairs of presidential candidates, as though such information was vitally important to the consideration of their official qualifications. Another mixed message is being presented when subtle as well as blatant sexual involvements are legally allowed on television in the name of free speech, but a political candidate's private life including his or her sex life is considered "open game" for the media to discover and, more importantly, to criticize.

A third form of mixed message has recently developed in the entertainment industry. It involves music groups who lip-synch songs while posing as the real vocal artist without public knowledge of the fraudulent activity. The pop music duo, Milli Vanilli, is an example of famous entertainers who acted like their voices were those that were actually recorded. However. several other groups in the past did the same thing on some or all of what were alleged to be "their" hits (Freund, 1990, E1). While such a hoax would not normally be considered in the "earth-shattering" category of news, it serves as another example to children that fraud is okay if you can get away with it. It is also another example presented to youth of "What you see is not necessarily what you get, and that's okay if they can get away with it."

Problems of Socialization and Social Capital

Problems of socializing our youth are further exacerbated by the hedonistic practices which have developed over the last quarter-century in our culture. A good summary of the profuse number of challenges we face in the socialization process today is presented by Marian Wright Edelman, president of the Children's Defense Fund:

> Our children are growing up today in an ethically polluted nation where instant sex without responsibility, instant gratification without effort, instant solutions without sacrifice, getting rather than giving, and hoarding rather than sharing are the too-frequent signals of our mass media, popular culture, business, and political life...Nowhere is the paralysis of public and private conscience more evident than in the neglect and abandonment of millions of our shrinking pool of children, whose future will determine our nation's ability to lead in a new era (O'Neil, 1991, 4).

Dr. James Coleman, professor of sociology at the University of Chicago, claims that our contemporary dilemma of youth problems is resulting in a depletion of what he calls "social capital." By "social capital," he means the resources needed for effective adaptation in society: norms, values, and the various human experiences and skills available only from trustworthy adults. And, according to Coleman, this decline of such important social "assets" is occurring because more and more youth are increasingly being denied important support and direction from significant adults during their transition from childhood through adolescence to adulthood.

In addition, children end up as the primary victims of broken homes caused by the over-fifty percent rate of divorce each year. We also have an annual increase in the reported number of child-abuse cases and children living in poor conditions. Many more of these unfortunate cases supposedly exist as well, but are not reported (according to experts in social problems). All in all, social capital, to use Professor Coleman's term, continues to be dramatically drained each year in our country by these types of disruptive occurrences (O'Neil, 1991, 7).

As our social capital continues to decrease, the steady rise in teenage gangs and youth violence become more understandable. As I described in chapter 1, affiliation with other youth in a gang at least provides camaraderie, the feeling of belonging and being wanted, as well as a sense of security that might otherwise be missing. A gang becomes somewhat of a surrogate family and helps the youth avoid the worst of feelings: insecurity and alienation.

Reverend Gregory Boyle (1990), a Jesuit priest and former pastor of Dolores Mission Catholic Church in East Los Angeles, identifies the core of despair that so many of our youth feel today, which prompts them to join teen gangs. Being familiar with so many of these young gang members, he speaks of their needs knowledgeably. He identifies lack of alternative activities as being a significant factor leading to gang involvement. He claims that the answer is decidedly not more police force action. Rather, the problem will continue as long as there are no other alternative activities for these youth. While Father Boyle believes that an increase in the number of jobs is the number one solution, the problem as he describes it highlights the lack of appropriate alternative activities for this population.

Of course, there is a twofold price to be paid for this family proxy, the teen gang. The first price is paid by the individual gang members. Each of them lose time and energy which could be devoted to developmental activities in educational or other constructive pursuits. Yet pointing out such heavy "prices" to gang members falls on deaf ears when they see themselves having no alternatives for affiliation and support.

The other price is paid by all of us, in both direct and indirect costs. Such costs include but are not limited to the following: loss of lives and property destruction due to gang violence, lost production by gang members who otherwise might be gainfully employed and/or enrolled in educational programs in preparation for later productive work, and costs for law enforcement agencies involved in investigating and apprehending youth offenders of the law, as well as preventive and remedial services of the juvenile justice system.

The "Sacred" vs. the "Profane"

James Spencer and James Barth (1992) provide valuable observations regarding the decreased sense of norms among many of our youth. The decrease in social capital discussed above has led to a growing inability in youth to distinguish the profane from the sacred. When everything can be cast into the category of relevancy, there is no standard rule to follow in making behavioral judgments. Standards of right or wrong eventually become completely subject to individual interpretation instead of being applicable to all.

This was one of the greatest concerns of our nation's founding fathers. They intended that our republic be ruled by law, not individual men. In addition to their observations of the despotic tendencies of individuals given unlimited power, they were also aware of what Spencer and Barth remind us about past civilizations which adapted the philosophy of relevancy: they did not survive long afterwards. Spencer and Barth (13) help us clarify our situation:

> There was a time that schools, and history classes in particular, were places where adolescents could safely challenge adult ways of thinking and questioning. They could question events and issues and form their own conclusions within the confines of some sort of orthodoxy. The orthodoxy, although vague at times, held that some standard of good and evil existed, that there is a difference between proper and improper behavior, and that some lines simply are not to be crossed.

Things are different today, though, according to Spencer and Barth. Many adolescents either lack an explicit system of beliefs and standards of behavior or have, at best, a very confused set of behavior standards.

N. C. WESLEYAN COLLEGE
ELIZABETH BRASWELL PEARSALL LIB

These suggestions are certainly corroborated by the statistics of juvenile delinquency (Spencer & Barth, 1992, 13).

We can gain some insight as to how such an attitude is encouraged in youth of today by considering the philosophy of the programming of MTV, one of the most popular television networks among youth today as described by Ron Powers (1990, 25) in his book, *The Beast, The Eunuch, And The Glass-Eyed Child, Television in the '80's:*

> (MTV) liberated television itself from orthodox meaning...The meaning of time, or narrative, or paradox, or necessity, (or) cause and effect...eliminated the sacred and the profane ...and authority as represented by school teachers, policemen, clergy. And parents.
>
> Powers quotes the founder of MTV, Robert Pittman: This (today's youth) is a non-narrative generation. You communicate to them via the sense impressions. There are two groups of people in this world: those who grew up with television and those who didn't grow up with sense impressions.

There appears to be a parallel between that philosophy and the breakdown in youth belief systems and behavior standards. Powers' statement says it all. Evidently, MTV's programming, as intended by Pittman, attempts to contradict standards of belief and behavior, and encourages self-indulgent attitudes which spring from promoting the philosophy of satisfying one's sensual instincts above any other. Statistical findings of studies, such as the Johns Hopkins University survey regarding the high percentage of Maryland eighth graders involved in explicit sex cited earlier in this chapter, certainly correlate positively with Pittman's philosophy.

In lieu of continuing erosion of the family unit and proliferation of mixed messages in our society today, is there any doubt that strong alternative programs are needed to give youth a sense of structure, direction, and a sense of right or wrong? Professor William Kilpatrick provides valuable perspective regarding such a "free-floating," relativistic and self-centered philosophy. He emphasizes the need for youth to receive direction regarding moral standards from the adults of a free society. While we will review the significance of activities which promote community in chapter 6, Kilpatrick (1992) focuses the lense on the need for a commonly practiced set of moral principles in a democracy. His expose of the relativistic and self-centered philosophy of Friedrich Nietzsche greatly resembles that of MTV:

> What is good? asks Nietzsche.—All that heightens the feeling of power, the will to power, power itself in man. What is bad?—All that proceeds from weakness....Prior to Nietzsche, philosophers had always tried to justify moral decisions in reference to something else—either to God or natural reason or nature. With Nietzsche, decisions become self-legitimating. An exercise of the will justifies itself just like an exercise on the high bar. One does it because one has the strength to do it, and because it is to exercise one's powers to the fullest. Since, from Nietzschean viewpoint, there are no external standards, the point is not what you choose, the point is choose daringly and wholeheartedly. Nowadays we would call it being authentic...(155-156).

It is helpful to our understanding of youth problems to know that MTV's is the programming philosophy is what underlies what many, if not most, of our youth embrace as worthwhile entertainment. When we add the continuing erosion of the family and the other social ills discussed above, there is little wonder why we continue to see behavior reflecting confused set of norms among our youth: an ever increasing state of anomie. How do young people choose one set of actions over another if they have little or no direction as to what is good (sacred) and what is not (profane)? If youth are constantly exposed to mixed messages about what is socially acceptable behavior versus that which is anti-social, how do they make sense out of those messages?

Sports: No Mixed Messages!

Sports provide popular types of activity in our society that hold out a strong alternative to others that are pervaded by mixed messages. In these activities, students have modeled for them clear examples of people working together and in competition against others with the same type of equipment, clothing, and under the same rules which are equally enforced during the contest. The goals and rules are clearly established for all to observe and rules are formally enforced by a neutral third party (the official) as stipulated in a formally printed rule book. There are no mixed messages on the field or court of play. During a sports contest, student-participants are presented rules that are defined and sanctions that are enforced immediately upon violation of those rules.

In school sports, we have demonstrated before us a model of human interactions regulated by official standards as well as an unwritten code of acceptable behavior. They present an ideal of what one sees and hears as reality, i.e., what you see and hear is what you actually get, instead of confusion and doubt resulting from mixed messages. The ideal is on display for all to see, relate to, and understand. An ideal of correct versus incorrect behavior according to socially prescribed rules is presented, reinforcing our sense of justice. It is an ideal that distinguishes "sacred" (acceptable) from "profane" (incorrect or unacceptable) behavior; a distinction that underpins all normative rules for the members of all societies. Particularly, it is a model of defined rules fairly enforced for community living. It provides behavior standards which, if violated, carry negative consequences for those who violate them. Finally, all observers are aware of the positive consequences when rule infractions are avoided.

The challenging subject of how to counteract mixed messages is a gigantic social and political monster that will call on the efforts of leaders from all segments of our society. Yet, our major institution for the socialization of our young, our schools, have the means, in the scholastic-co-curricular activities model, to influence positive changes. Unfortunately, over the past 25 years, we have decreased this capacity, and now we have the predictable negative results.

We truly find ourselves in a paradox regarding our nation's youth, who comprise our nation's future. While youth gangs and crime dramatically increase, schools are forced to cut back on various academic and co-curricular programs including professionally trained counselors, coaches and moderators.

By undercutting such valuable educational programs, we are letting slip right through our societal fingers the most important means of socialization of our youth. After a few hundred years of evolution and maturation, America's educational system had developed basic structures which helped youth develop important academic, physical, and vocational abilities and social values, including those of citizenship. Like any human institution, American schools have never reached perfection in the complete socialization of all our youth. There is always room for improvement. Fortunately, however, required classroom learning and voluntary participation in the academic-co-curricular model of education and socialization provided an effective process of socialization, which accommodated a myriad of differences required in a pluralistic democratic society. Unfortunately, this basic academic-co-curricular model has been eroded in its potential to assist youth in their personal and interpersonal development.

American education is currently in a well-publicized crisis because of declining achievement scores, and decreased funding, resulting in cutbacks or complete elimination of valuable educational programs and teaching positions. At a time when more good teachers and quality programs are needed to meet growing needs of our youth, funding is being slashed. With Owen Davies, well-known scientific forecaster of social and economic trends, Dr. Marvin Cetron (Cetron & Davies, 1989) presents budget statistics which help to clarify the need for more educational funding.

> For a start, if we really want quality education in United States, we have to be willing to pay for it. In recent years, we haven't been. Even after the National Commission on Excellence in Education published its landmark report, A *Nation at Risk*, in 1983, the Reagan administration never asked for a significant increase in federal aid to education. In fact, the White House attempted to cut the national education budget by over $10 billion, after inflation. Congress always restored most of those cuts, so that federal education spending still totaled about $19.5 billion in 1986. Yet by 1988 the federal government was actually spending about 14 percent less for education (in constant dollars) than it had five years earlier. Given such circumstances, it is no surprise that teachers are still dramatically underpaid when compared with other professions that require a college education. In 1987, the average starting salary for an accountant was $21,200, beginning computer specialists received $26,170, and new engineers took in $28,500. The average starting salary for a teacher was only $17,500. In forty out of fifty states, a starting garbage collector makes more money than a starting teacher (53)...Where broken homes are the rule, and parents themselves have little respect for education, teachers must provide the individual attention that parents do not. In crowded classrooms, they can't do it (54).

Among the most important of the programs first cut from school's budgets are co-curricular activities. As pointed out by Cetron and Davies, the corrective actions we need to take to improve American education is to increase financial and any other viable means of support to all areas of education, particularly on the elementary and secondary levels. But, in so doing, we need to realize the significance of both co-curricular and core academic subject areas and their complimentary effects on American students.

We can feel optimistic that in school sports and other co-curricular activities, we have available the means to reinforce classroom programs as well as provide youth with voluntary involvements that contribute to their democratic socialization. The focus of this book is on the reasons for such optimism.

School Sports: Beyond Fun and Games

Again, school sports, more than any other single type of activity, promote and reinforce the principles of the United States Constitution and our democratic way of life. No other single type of activity brings together people from completely different social, economic, political, religious, and racial backgrounds to participate in common, directly or indirectly, as school sports and other co-curricular activities. They are freely chosen by students; students are not required to participate, as they are required to do in the classroom. They all provide students with opportunities to commit themselves voluntarily to something larger than their own immediate needs and wants. Students are provided the opportunity to concurrently practice personal initiative with cooperation in this non-required activity. Whether direct competition is involved or not, students have opportunities to experience and deal with successes and disappointments that result from their efforts alone and in cooperation with others.

So, why have we been decreasing rather than increasing support for these educational activities? Why have we de-emphasized these programs which so wonderfully supported democratic ideals for so many years? Why are we limiting the hope of so many young people as well as the numerous benefits to our nation by forsaking the quantity and quality of our school sports and other co-curricular programs in America?

These are important questions when we consider that, as support for these voluntary educational programs has been increasingly cut back over the past 25 years, our youth problems have increased drastically. As we further discuss in subsequent chapters the great value of these voluntary programs in American education and socialization, it will be helpful to us to keep these questions in mind.

Chapter 3

Sports & Competition: Their Value to Western Civilization, Education, & Democracy

> The adult world is...built on the shifting ground of friendship and competition. The double message of this society and economy are to get along and get ahead. We want our children to fit in and stand out. We rarely address the conflict between these goals. - Ellen Goodman, "Old Friendship and Competition," Washington Post, 1986

As we will discuss in more detail in chapter 4, unpredictable events of this world cause the grounds of our lives to frequently shift all around us, and we must learn to adapt. Life involves continuous adaptations to the unexpected, including the winds of change within relationships as well as within oneself. Although we hope that our children will adapt effectively early in their lives, a main task of growing older is to continue learning the ways of adaptation. The processes of education and socialization are intended to prepare young people to assume roles of increasing responsibility, roles that will be greatly based on their ability to adjust to life's challenges, both anticipated and unexpected.

While the classroom provides good opportunities for youth to acquire information about people, our world, and our society, the classroom learning experience is also mandated: youth have no choice in attending. Although we intend and hope that the classroom teacher will be able to develop a course interesting in content and format and will also be able to motivate students to want to learn the material, attendance is still mandatory.

In contrast, youth participate in co-curricular programs voluntarily. They involve themselves, by choice, with others in cooperative and competitive efforts. It is very important that students learn to cooperate and compete, when and where it is appropriate, in both the required classroom as well as in voluntary co-curricular learning experiences. Both learning experiences are significant to the education and socialization of young people as they learn to adapt to a democratic society in which citizens choose to participate and interact daily with each other.

Increased Cooperation: Concomitant of Competition

Cooperation has been more operative in the completion of most human accomplishments than competition, and it is fundamental to the survival of a democratic nation. Great achievements, whether in the areas of architecture, business, sports, education, war, or any other pursuit, have resulted far more from cooperative efforts than aggressive competition among or between people. Yet the cooperative effort is heightened and intensified when the results of one group's efforts are pitted against those of another group, as done every day throughout the United States and other nations with free enterprise economies. This is the operative principle every time one manufacturer tries to produce a better version of a particular product than another manufacturing firm for the same or less cost; or whenever one prospective job hunter attempts to be hired by an employer over another applicant.

Both competition and cooperation have always played favorable roles in the evolution of the United States. Of the many attributes used to describe early Americans and pioneers who settled the western territory, "competitive spirit" is undoubtedly one of the most fitting. Whether early settlers were struggling against the often dangerous forces of nature, the resistance of native American Indians, pioneers from other competing foreign lands, or their own internal conflicts, they had to fight their way through.

Competition is inherent in a society with a free enterprise economic system such as our own in the United States. It is a necessary activity that acts as the basis of our call from Thomas Jefferson to "pursue life, liberty, and happiness" when he authored the Declaration of Independence. Yet detractors of competition protest that it promotes division and violence more than any positive outcomes. Such negative perceptions are usually held by people who have observed others engage in competition with apparent destructive intentions.

Like most anything else, though, competition can be negative or positive, depending on how it is learned and conducted. This point in itself is reason enough to instruct our youth in constructive approaches to competition during their middle and high school years, as they prepare for a career in our competition-based free enterprise system. Competition should be taught and learned in positive ways during these formative years. The key precautions against destructive forms of competition are enforced laws against such improper conduct, and education of our youth in constructive forms of competition. School sports and other co-curricular programs provide youth with voluntary experiences in the practice of constructive competitive procedures in areas of natural interest to them under the guidance of adult mentors.

To help us clarify how, as experienced in school sports, competition actually enhances cooperative activities let us now consider the correlation from a few historical as well as contemporary perspectives.

What is Competition and From Whence it Came?

What is the object of competition? Its most basic purpose is striving to accomplish a particular objective, which could be acquisition of a predetermined reward, surpassing a previous record, winning a contest, or resolving a conflict. Competition most commonly is thought to involve one person or group in a combative struggle with another individual or group. However, competition does not begin with one person vying with another.

The first and most important form of competition takes place within oneself. It originates in the pull we each feel between one internal "voice" which tells a person to do one thing and another or more "voices" instructing or even demanding that same person to take some other action. No matter what society or economic system one lives in, he or she is daily confronted with this internal struggle. Learning how to constructively reconcile these internal opposing forces is basic to the human condition.

In addition to this innate internal competition, man has had to be an external competitor as long as he has existed. In his earliest experiences, he had to compete against the forces of nature. In his primal years of development, man constantly had to escape life-threatening predators or compete with other animals for food and, later, land to farm. Survival was dependent on his ability to compete.

As groups of men eventually developed rivalries against other groups for the means of subsistence, those who brought home the biggest or the best of the spoils won in competition over others received the greatest rewards from their tribe. Superior catches of food or other valued materials were acclaimed more than lesser ones. Eventually individuals learned that larger rewards were available by combining their lone efforts with those of others. Hence was born the original concept of the "team" effort.

Eventually, man came to associate good and bad events in life with good and evil spirits. As a result, he developed physical contests through which he believed he could win the favor and assistance of the good spirits against the evil forces. Such ceremonial events were later developed into more sophisticated ritual athletic contests, as performed in ancient Egypt and Greece. Athletic contests, including various feats of strength and foot races, eventually became ritualized and ceremonial in the worship of their gods. It was even thought that one could secure immortality by performing record feats in athletic contests.

Competition & Community

Thus, physical excellence and superior athletic skills came to be highly valued and considered to one of man's great goals. These qualities also came to be considered among the main foundations for a strong and vigorous country. Such was the elevation of sports-related abilities in the earliest of democratic states on record, Greece. More than 2,500 years ago, men from all corners of Greece would come together at the sacred grove of Olympia to compete in the most famous athletic contests in history, the Olympic games. Revived in 1896, this international athletic event is now conducted every four years.

No other single type of activity brings together people from completely different segments of our culture in common as sports, particularly school sports. Even in early days of civilization, harmony was facilitated by sports contests which actually acted as bridges to temporary peace between warring parties. During these athletic contests, a truce of peace was honored by all city states of the Greek world. The best athletes of that time competed in various athletic contests such as boxing, wrestling, and different types of racing events between men on foot, on horseback, and in chariots. When the winners returned to their homelands to present their crowns of victory in their respective temples, they would be welcomed back as heroes by their fellow citizens. (For a more complete discussion of the historical roots of sports and competition, see Baker, 1988, Mandell, 1988, and Guttman, 1978.)

We can see that competitive sports activities have existed as a form of recreation and pastime since man's beginnings, and have been highly regarded as worthwhile functions in the earliest civilizations. Civilizations which developed many of our most honored traditions in philosophy, government, and art also placed a high value in physical strength and skills. They were considered to be an integral part of overall well-being, and have thus become part of Western traditions. We can also understand that, properly introduced and taught to our own citizens during the socialization process, and consistently monitored for appropriate conduct according to equally enforced rules, physical activities can be stimulants for personal effort and interpersonal bonds. Again, the key is how competition is introduced to and learned by citizens, and then how how it is regulated according to law.

Competition & Democracy

Two of the leading western political theorists who influenced the thinking of the founding fathers of our Constitution held extremely opposite views regarding man's nature as it relates to the issue of competition. Jean Jacques Rousseau, one of the leaders of the French Revolution, believed that man is naturally peaceful whose primary tendency is to seek harmony with nature. He thought that men are only corrupted by the various entrapments and comforts that derive from civilization. On the other hand, the Englishman, Thomas Hobbes contended that man is selfish by nature and acts primarily to satisfy his own concerns before helping others. While Rousseau believed that cooperation is man's natural bent, Hobbes thought that man is naturally competitive.

In their book, *Struggle For Democracy*, Benjamin Barber and Patrick Watson (1980) review common as well as divergent factors that have influenced the formation and maintenance of democracies throughout history. They claim that:

> It is when we turn to look at people from the inside that we find both Hobbes and Rousseau were right...the struggle for democracy also turns out to be a struggle within ourselves: it is a tension we see quite clearly in children between yearning for freedom and...security, the need to govern ourselves and the need to be taken care of by others, the need to give and the need to take (xv-xviii).

Again, it is indeed true that competition begins within the individual - within each of us - before it is evidenced or exhibited externally against another. For we compete daily with ourselves in making one choice over another. In the extreme, we might experience an intense internal conflict in choosing to act contrary to what we want to do in favor of another. Or, in lesser extreme, we feel a slight tension in making such decisions.

Sports & Competition: Their Value to American Democracy

Ultimately, the Constitution integrates both Hobbes' competitive and Rousseau's cooperative views in a paradoxical effort to combine individual interests and rights with the overall needs and claims of the community. The freedoms of the individual are provided for within the common good of all citizens. This proposed compromise to simultaneously honor and protect both individual freedoms and the best interests of the community was a difficult endeavor. That is why the Constitution was termed from its beginning as a political "experiment" - an experiment which is now over 200 years old.

As uncomfortable as it may be to some, tension generated by competitive and cooperative forces paradoxically underpins our Constitution: individual equality and rights are prized above all other issues within the overall needs and concerns of the community. This divalent principle, although anchored and reinforced by law and our justice system, necessarily thrives because of the dichotomous tension inherent in the co-relationship of individual rights and group claims. While the interconnection between these two ideas is taut by nature, it has been made flexible by the wise provisions written into the Constitution by the founding fathers: a system of fundamental law, checks and balances of government, and provision for its amendment.

In other words, the natural competition inherent in the duadic principle of our democracy is made to work by the ongoing system of debate, agreement to disagree, and compromise by vote. Agreement is reached as provided by law which is ultimately determined by vote of the individuals who comprise the group. Competing views held by different citizens are debated and finally resolved by majority vote. In this political process voluntary commitment and proactivity are important attributes to be practiced by the citizens of a democracy. And these attributes are regularly practiced in school co-curricular programs.

Competition and cooperation: both are fundamental to democracy. And it is very important in our free enterprise economic system that these principles be properly integrated and practiced by citizens as part of the socialization process within our schools.

Competition is at the very base of our political system of electing officials. No matter what funding limits or other rules are set down in an election, one candidate challenges another to win the election. To win a political election means for one candidate to earn more points, or rather, votes, than another. It is competition in its essence. Our democratic electoral process must involve competition.

This dynamic relationship of competition and cooperation is regularly replicated and modeled for us during sports activities. In *Take Time for Paradise*, the late former Yale University president and Commissioner of Major League Baseball, Dr. A. Bartlett Giamatti (1990, 50-67) gives an incisive commentary as to how this dynamic is constructively modeled in sports. Although there are two opponents, each competing for victory over the other, both are in agreement as to the rules which will decide who, in fact, does win at the end of the contest. The competition always ends in agreement - a positive form of resolution. And all this competition takes place - with final resolution according to agreement - in an activity in which there is no ultimate outcome except to pursue self-improvement and contribute to that of the team. Further, there is immediate feedback as to one's actions.

In this way, American sports contribute greatly to the ongoing interplay of the principles of the Constitution and continuance of our democracy. We can better understand this dynamic if we take a look at the evolution of sports activities and how they have come to align with that of social and political developments in America.

Origins of American Sports Popularity

The genesis of modern-day American sports actually began in eighteenth-century England. Much of the growth of American sports as we know them today coincides with developments in social, political, and industrial circumstances occurring in England. Eventually, sports participation was embraced by Americans with the same passion that they pursued the settlement of the western part of the United States.

Several aspects of modern sports actually were rooted in the advancements made in manufacturing in England, which were the same developments that gave birth to our industrial revolution. Techniques such as standardization, specialization, and regulation were employed for greater efficiency in the manufacture of tools and other products. Such techniques facilitated more specific measurement, and the development of interchangeable parts which could be more easily assembled. These same procedures also revolutionized sports.

Although sports such as boxing and foot races were traditional athletic contests in England and elsewhere in Europe, there were few standards or regulations regarding time and distance. Following the employment of the new industrial measurement techniques for manufacturing, written rules of various standards were established in sports. In track, for example, specific distances were determined for foot races, the shot put was set at 16 pounds, and events such as the low and high hurdles with specified distances and heights were established. Another example was the emergence of specified limits on time per round and number of rounds comprising a match or contest in boxing and wrestling. Also, body weight classifications and rules for the conduct of participants were set down in writing for these sports.

The introduction of sports programs to the curricula of public schools first took place in mid-1800's England. It actually occurred following changes taking place in the structure of sports play, mentioned above, and socio-political changes which were simultaneously occurring. When Parliament's power increased while that of King George III decreased in the late 1800's, common people in England achieved greater say in government, and the lower classes began to participate in sports more frequently. Standard measurements and regulations provided a common basis for them to participate and compete with those of the gentry classes. As sports participation became significantly more popular and widespread among all social classes, barriers to interactions between lower and upper classes became less apparent. This historical development is an example of the power of sports to break down social barriers among people, and how athletics participation can strongly promote and reinforce principles of democracy. (Again, for a detailed history of the evolution of Western European and American sports, see Baker, 1988, Mandell, 1988, and Guttman 1978.)

Beginnings of Co-curricula Programs in American Schools

Among the most notable of our nation's founding fathers who believed that an educated citizenry is required for democracy to survive were George Washington, James Madison, Benjamin Franklin, and Thomas Jefferson. Jefferson strongly supported the Northwest Ordinance of 1787 requirement that each township created by the Land Ordinance of 1785 provide a square mile of land for educational purposes. Later, during the presidential administration of Andrew Jackson in the 1830's, the popularity of publicly-supported education spread considerably. It was held that a system of publicly supported education of all youth, rich or poor, would help equalize opportunities for all citizens to participate in the democratic social order.

As this philosophy among national leaders developed further, schools eventually became the chief agency not only for formal education, but also for the general socialization of young people. And, indeed, there was need of such a societal agency, as problems among youth began to dramatically increase with the extensive influx of immigrants and farmers during the late 1800's.

Formal schools, both private and publicly supported, were founded in early colonial days, beginning in Massachusetts in the 1647, and gradually proliferated through the beginning of our republic. Schools as we think of them today, though, had their roots mainly in those established during the nineteenth century. Formal attendance requirements were not even put into force until the late 1800's. As industrial advancements continued to be made during the 1800's, Horace Mann and social scientists called for the school curriculum to include vocational training to prepare students for the workplace. This was seen as a means to decrease social conflicts as more citizens would leave school prepared to contribute productively to society.

Meanwhile, the U.S. experienced a tremendous transformation from being primarily a rural society to an urban society. Greater job opportunities developed by the industrialization process prompted millions of people to move from farms to the cities. Approximately 26 million immigrants between 1870-1920 further increased the urbanization of America during this period. As immigrants tended to congregate with people from their original country, different ethnic neighborhoods developed, which precipitated conflicts among these groups. The greatest prevalence of such ethnic conflicts occurred among youth gangs.

Although sweeping industrialization in America was tabbed as the culprit in this increase in youth problems at the turn of the century, there is a considerable similarity between such problems then and those of today, as evidenced by the following observation made in 1904 by Robert Hunter, who is quoted by University of California at Berkeley history professor, Paula Fass (1989, 13), in her book *Outside In: Minorities and the Transformation of American Education*:

> These present-day problems of the child - the cities, the coming of immigrants, the collapse of homelife, the yardless tenement - all are due to one underlying cause. There has been an entire revolution in industry during the last century, and nearly all the problems of child life have grown up as a result of this revolution.

Although this statement was made in 1904, it generally applies to the situation of our youth problems today. And, it was largely due to the problems of youth as perceived across the country that measures were taken to accelerate both the attendance of children in schools and the socialization role with which schools came to be associated. As also quoted by Professor Fass (13), education historian Carl F. Kaestle provides additional insight:

> ...schooling for early nineteenth century Americans was intended to be a broadly socializing experience. The hoped- for outcomes included high-minded character, a religiously derived morality, and industriousness oriented to social   progress - virtues understood to be essential to effective republican citizenship. 'The chief end is to make GOOD CITIZENS,' an Illinois superintendent maintained at mid-century. 'Not to make precocious scholars...not to impart the secret of acquiring wealth...not to qualify directly for professional success...but simply to make good citizens.' Toward this end, reformers labored to make at least a limited exposure to publicly supported schools the common possession of most Americans. Even the exceptions (at that time) - Blacks, Asians, Indians, whose relation to the republic was highly problematic - emphasized the inclusive goals of the ideology for those who were potential constituents of the civic society and contributed to its policy.'

The evolution and importance of co-curricular activities, including school sports, coincide with the evolution of American education in general and, in particular, the high school in our country. The idea of social efficiency was central to the development of the high school at the turn of the century and continued through the mid-1950's. In addition to preparing an individual youth to do a postgraduate job well, social efficiency meant learning to get along well with others. Put into practice, it was thought that the high school curriculum should include activities to help young people develop social skills so that they could become participating and contributing citizens. In other words, America had come to be see schools as responsible for students' development of citizenship skills, as well as literacy skills.

Spring (1986, 201) points out that, at the turn of the century, "adolescence was seen as the most important age for developing a sense of cooperation and social service required by modern society." Adolescence at this time was viewed as being a period of life during which an individual would develop the behaviors that, in turn, would determine his ultimate life direction: "...youth represented either a promising future or a collapsing civilization" (201). It was this prophetic image of youth that most influenced the development in America of what is referred to as the comprehensive high school. This perspective was also the primary factor in the development of co-curricular activities in schools.

Largely due to this popularized image of youth being "the most important age for developing a sense of cooperation and socialization" as suggested by Spring, schools became synonymous with a hopeful future for America. That is, the schools and the responsibility they were given in the development of the habits and characteristics of youth were thought to be primary in the maintenance and promotion of our American democratic society.

Socialization & Co-curricular Programs

This philosophy, in which schools held center stage in the socialization of youth, was most specifically reflected in a report called the "Cardinal Principles of Secondary Education," issued in 1918 by the Commission on the Reorganization of Secondary Education. The report suggested, in addition to providing practical courses to help students perform industrial jobs well, that the secondary school curriculum provide common activities to promote unification of citizens. Sound familiar? Concerns for developing community were strongly voiced back then! Things have not changed relative to the need for common activities which promote unity. There is as much need today as ever before, as our national population becomes increasingly pluralistic.

The report goes on to underscore the need for unifying activities in schools:

> The purpose of democracy is so to organize society so that each member may develop his personality primarily through activities designed for the well-being of his fellow members and of society as a whole...education in a democracy...should develop in each individual the knowledge, interests, ideals, habits, and powers whereby he will find his place and use that place to shape both himself and society toward ever nobler ends (Spring, 1986, 203).

Following the suggestions of the Commission's "Cardinal Principles of Secondary Education" report, co-curricular activities were more widely instituted and emphasized.

Activities in which people of any and all backgrounds were voluntarily involved together towards achieving a common goal or task have been most influential in the promotion and maintenance of our democratic society. The Constitution's final acceptance was based on compromise among delegates from each state, following mutual interchange and debate at the Constitutional Convention. It was the common interest among those delegates that the new republic would be governed, not by men, but rather by law which gave birth to the final document on which our country is based. As a result, there will always be a need for activities such as co-curricular programs which promote common voluntary involvements. And such programs will always be as important as the "core" curriculum in schools within a democracy.

Co-curricular programs facilitate common involvements on a voluntary basis; people become involved with each other based on freely chosen interests rather than required academic course subjects. In practice, each participant strives to improve his or her individual skills while competing against his or her teammates. In the process, he or she learns that his or her own successful efforts are enhanced when they also contribute to the success of the group, the team. In addition, they have an overall objective, outperforming an opposing team from another school which provides still another measure for them to gauge their efforts. All the while, the members of a team or any other activity practice cooperation in striving for their individual and mutual improvement. All for one, one for all: the essence of team...one of the main reasons youth resort to gang membership when constructive alternatives are not available.

Youth are looking for direction and for ways to feel viable, to become empowered. Gangs have been offering these opportunities where youth otherwise have no other options. As youth attempt to deal with the constant changes that life presents, they need alternative activities which constructively help them both to deal with the daily internal competition we all face and to develop their interests and themselves.

There can be no democracy without competition in politics, in business, or in various individual pursuits. It is of utmost importance to provide opportunities for youth to learn and practice positive, appropriate forms of competition. In so doing, they also learn the critical ability of cooperation! School sports and other co-curricular activities provide excellent means by which youth can learn both fair and appropriate competition and the skills of collaboration. Every day, our youth show up at our schools. Where better can such activities be taught and supervised by qualified mentors, and be used to encourage and reinforce study of core curricular subjects, than within our primary institutions of learning: our schools?

Having reviewed the importance of both competition and cooperation to America as constructively promoted by school co-curricular activities, we will now focus on how these educational programs help youth to learn proactive adaptation to life changes. Success or even survival in any phase of life requires proactive adaptation. In chapter 4, we will consider how school sports and other co-curricular programs help youth learn to be proactive in adapting to life changes involved in both cooperative and competitive activities.

Chapter 4

Dance of Life, Change, Adaptation & Empowerment

> Change is the law of life. And those who look only to the
> past or the present are certain to miss the future. - John F. Kennedy

President Kennedy's words were anticipated over 2,500 years ago by the Roman philosopher, Heraclitus, who claimed that there was only one permanent phenomenon in this world: change. It's the one occurrence we can count on no matter what else happens in our lives. Although it takes place in varying degrees as the seconds of our lives move along, change is in constant motion, like Oscar Hammerstein's "Ol' Man River."

Life is synonymous with change. As we discussed in chapter 3, we have to adapt to changes if we are to continue our lives. Life is a "dance," involving us in interactions and adaptations with continuous, fluctuating changes.

In his classic book, *Future Shock*, Alvin Toffler (1970, 1) tells us change is "the process by which the future invades our lives" and that its rate is continually increasing due to geometric technological advancements. Adaptation becomes even more complex in our country as our population becomes increasingly multicultural, and with the continued shift in demographics, rapidly changing economic and occupational conditions, breakdown of the family, increased crime and violence in our country, and ongoing global conflicts, the need to adapt grows greater daily.

The "dance of life" is becoming more challenging as human relationships have become more vulnerable to dissolution. This is particularly true for youth. Having a sense of stability and continuity is extremely important to youth in their efforts to successfully adapt to the daily "dance of life." Unfortunately, the continued breakdown of the family unit has contributed greatly to a growing sense of transience and instability.

Perceptions of rootlessness and uncertainty negatively influence how a person sees himself in relation to the future, and play a significant role in how well he adjusts to life changes. This is particularly true for children and adolescents, who are still formulating their overall perspectives of themselves and their world. To help us clarify this point, Toffler cites observations of Dr. Benjamin Singer, specialist in social psychiatry at the University of Western Ontario. According to Singer, each child carries in his mind not only an image of himself, a self-image, at the present moment; each child also has a set of mental pictures of himself as he wishes to be in the future:

> This person of the future provides a focus for the child; it is a magnet toward which he is drawn; the framework for the present, one might say, is created by the future (Toffler, 1971, 421).

Toffler (423) contends that for children to become more adaptable to their world of accelerating changes, "We must sensitize them to the possibilities and probabilities of tomorrow. We must enhance their sense of the future."

Important information which complements Singer's claims has been provided by studies conducted by leading psychologist and University of Pennsylvania professor, Martin E.P. Seligman, and his colleagues. The results of these investigations of motivational factors further help us to identify the importance of one's self-concept, self-confidence, and the value of school sports in helping youth develop adaptational skills and a sense of personal efficacy. According to these findings, apart from a mere lack of interest in a particular activity, motivational deficits are primarily due to a person's perception that he is unable to do anything to influence important events in his life. That is, when a person thinks that he has no power to affect certain circumstances in his life, he will avoid attempting to affect them (Seligman, 1975, 1991).

Thomas Peters and Robert Waterman (1982, 80) report that other psychologists have referred to this need for self-control as "illusion of control":

> ...findings [of these psychologists] indicate that if people think they have even modest personal control over their destinies, they will persist at tasks. They will do better at them. They will become more committed to them.

These and similar studies have shown that proactivity (i.e., action taken by a person on his own volition) tends to ward off negative self-perceptions of impotency and actually increase those of empowerment. Also, an individual tends to become empowered when he or she has a sense that his or her actions has potential to influence important events in her or his life. That is, people feel empowered when they believe that they have the ability to make a difference in their own lives and their community. The key to empowerment, then, is belief in one's own potential to take action. To become empowered, therefore, one needs to experience that his actions can influence desired outcomes.

These research findings support one's sense that if, in a person's experience he has never been able to affect his life changes except through violent or deviant behavior, that is what he will try to do to make a difference. If he believes that he has no way to improve his life circumstance other than affiliating with gangs, because that is the only thing he has experienced which in any way works, that is what he will do. Where survival depends on getting what you can immediately, such as the high from taking drugs or money from selling them, youth gravitate to those activities in which they can best secure survival now! Forget about what types of activities are best for them in the long run. If they have little or no prior exposure to alternative activities that "pay off" (help them to survive) in the long term, how are they to understand that hard work within the system (of society) can help them?

School Sports, Proactivity, Self-Confidence & Adaptation

Without constructive experiences and role models who genuinely care about youth, society's hope that significant changes in the behavior of wayward youth will occur is a pipe dream! Where the only survival skills that are modeled for youth are those involving deviant behavior, that is what youth tend to imitate. And we do not have to rely on advanced social science research to know this important information. American educators at the turn of the last century expressed this view, as mentioned in chapter 3

In 1903, New York City schools responded to the need for constructive youth activities by establishing the Public Schools Athletic League. In that year, President Theodore Roosevelt subsequently heralded the importance of that program in the following letter sent to its founder:

The great congestion in population has resulted in depriving the children of New York the opportunity to exercise so their physical development tends to drop below normal. The energies they should work off in wholesale exercise, in vigorous play, find vent in the worst feats of the gangs which represent so much that is vicious in our city life. It is a great disadvantage to a boy to be unable to play games; and every boy who knows how to play baseball, football, to box or wrestle, has by just so much fitted himself to a better citizen (DeFrantz, 1989).

Is there anything in this letter that sounds familiar about youth and city life today?

Stanford University psychologist, Albert Bandura, and other researchers have provided more substantial research evidence regarding the vital importance for constructive programs like co-curricular activities as alternatives to destructive activities. Bandura and his colleagues have demonstrated that the most effective method of learning is through example (i.e., a person learns best by imitating the effective performance of a task by another person). Bandura explains the findings of these studies as follows:

In actuality, virtually all learning phenomena resulting from direct experience occur on a vicarious basis by observing other people's behavior and its consequences for them. The capacity to learn by observation enables people to acquire large, integrated patterns of behavior without having to form them gradually by tedious trial and error (Waterman, 1986, 5).

Bandura's research findings, combined with those of Martin Seligman, help us to both make sense of how youth problems have increased so widely and to remind us of the valuable potential of school sports as constructive alternative activities. When youth are continually exposed to poor role models such as youth gang leaders and individual delinquents who, in fact, achieve "rewards" for participating in negative and anti-social behavior, why would we expect anything but such behavior to become a habit for youth who are not otherwise directed? Positive role models and constructive activities are vital for youth to learn appropriate and socially healthy habits, as well as self-confidence.

This point is further corroborated by Charles Garfield in his book, *Peak Performers*, in which he reports his findings from an 18 year study

of people who are consistent achievers in business. Over 300 peak performers included in Garfield's study claimed that they developed these traits
by watching other successful people. According to Garfield (1986, 16-19):

> One peak performer speaks for most others he replies, 'I got jump-
> started by watching others, by learning from the people I most admire.'
> The peak performers repeatedly say that stories of our most productive
> people provide them not only with strategies but also with values -
> values as leverage points for triggering that impulse to excel.

I believe that most readers would agree that young people who are
involved in constructive activities directed by caring educators/mentors
are more likely to develop positive behaviors than those involved in gangs
and other negative alternative engagements. One does not have to be
steeped in extensive social research findings to come to such a conclu-
sion. However, the above research findings, along with Garfield's observations of successful individuals learning effective behaviors by emulat-
ing other accomplished people, help reinforce the importance of constructive activities and role models. The voluntary educational activities
of school sports and other co-curricular programs provide such activities
to youth.

In addition to Garfield's observations and those of the studies noted
above, we can gain helpful insight about the development of empowering behaviors and adaptation to life changes from other people in successful organizations outside of education. Business firms, both large and
small, have to struggle constantly with the unexpected. Like most of us,
business firms are daily challenged by the perplexing changes inherent in
the "dance of life." Whether unforeseen problems involve personnel conflicts, breakdowns in production or communications, difficulties in col-
lecting receivable accounts, unhappy clients, or the myriad of other un-
anticipated adversities that frequently erupt in business situations, business leaders are constantly challenged to adjust to changing conditions,
and to empower their employees to do the same.

The value of discussing successful businesses is twofold. First, although business organizations ultimately involve groups of people responding and adapting to various demands placed on them, the organizational effort begins with multiple individual attempts to adapt within the
company. Subsequently, we are offered many examples of effective behaviors of numerous individuals responding concurrently, very similar to

the group dynamics which occur in school team sports and other co-curricular programs.

Second, as private businesses hire the majority of working people in America, it is important to see how school sports and other co-curricular programs strongly contribute to the preparation and development of youth in personal and interpersonal disciplines, as well as in the team experiences increasingly emphasized by business firms today.

Stochastic Changes & Renewing Companies

In his best-selling book, *The Renewal Factor*, Robert Waterman (1988) describes the characteristics common to companies who have consistent track records in effectively adapting to changes. He refers to these companies as "renewing companies," a name which underlines their admirable capacities to not only meet, but also to effectively anticipate, difficult changes.

Referring to the ongoing, unexpected and random conflicts that occur in the daily life of the business world as "stochastic shocks," Waterman (33) highlights their frequency:

"All too often [business organizations] get a sensible program going only to have it blown out of the water...by some capricious turn of the environment...some stochastic shock."

Of course, the same can be said of life in general! The dance of life is replete with stochastic shocks. Those who develop the means to cope with unexpected changes in the ebb and flow of life's unpredictable dance will be most successful in continuing or redirecting their life's course. Youth constantly face physiological and psychological changes which they have not experienced before, whether the changes are personal, interpersonal, within their families, or away from home. Adolescence is a critical time to have opportunities for constructive learning experiences in adapting to stochastic life changes. School sports and other co-curricular activities provide such opportunities to student-participants through the practice of the following principles of effective adaptation (all of which are among those common to renewing companies as described by Robert Waterman): having a sense of meaning through the pursuit of a mission and cultivating strong associations, flexible planning and having a sense of direction, stability in motion, persistence, continual measurement of performance, commitment, trust, and team.

In the balance of this balance, we will consider how each of these principles are similarly encouraged and practiced in school sports and other co-curricular program.

Mission & Meaning

Without an overall meaning, individuals as well as groups of people are less able to cope with change in general, and even less so with specific traumatic life circumstances. As indicated by the work of Martin Seligman discussed above, human beings are effectively empowered to adapt to life challenges when they perceive themselves as having the potential to do so. Having a mission enables a person to cope with and move through difficult situations; he is able to focus on the cause of his mission which supersedes his challenging conditions. Renewing companies engender optimistic attitudes among their people by establishing an organizational mission for all to keep at the forefront of their individual and collective thinking. Missions give life meaning to individuals and organizations as purpose is given to their thoughts and actions towards completion of the mission. The process of a person becoming empowered can be greatly enhanced when that individual believes his or her life has a meaning, a purpose.

The importance of having a sense of meaning is often overlooked in our materialistic society, particularly in its role during the socialization process. Dr. Victor Frankl provides us with insights as to how important this internal sense of purpose is. Frankl was an eminent psychiatrist in Vienna at the outbreak of World War II. He was one of the millions of Jews incarcerated in concentration camps, but one of the few to survive the heinous conditions of inhumane treatment at the hands of the German Nazis. In *Man's Search for Meaning*, Frankl describes the perilous suffering and decrepit conditions the Nazis inflicted on their Jewish captives. To survive such torture during the holocaust experience seems nothing short of luck or miraculous. Yet a few, including Frankl, did. But how? Or a better question still: *Why* did they survive?

According Dr. Frankl, those who survived longest before dying, and those who lived through the liberation of Europe by Allied forces, evidenced a sense of meaning and hope during their suffering. Such prisoners tended to be concerned about their fellow sufferers at least as much as they were with their own pain. As an example of such behavior among survivors, Dr. Frankl notes how they had voluntarily given their small piece of bread to another starving inmate who seemed to the giver (the survivor) as worse off than himself at the time. They regularly demonstrated self-sacrifice for the sake of their fellow prisoners at a time when they had little to give, other than an occasional bit of food or expression of concern.

Frankl's account of such courageous acts is testimony to the strength which mission and meaning can give to the lives of individuals and organizations. Missions and meaning engender powerful forces in the process of empowerment and acquiring hope - the main fuel of life. We know that if constructive alternative sources are not available, youth attempt to find meaning on their own - too often through self-defeating activities such as gang involvements. One way or another, youth seek to satisfy their need for meaning and associations. School sports and other co-curricular programs can provide a youth such meaning wherever there is a void in this area of his or her life. Or, co-curricular programs can add greater dimension to the life of a young person who is fortunate to have other sources of meaning.

Associations & Meaning

Most of us can easily relate to the added meaning that our associations with others can bring to life. If you recall that last time you were at a wake or funeral, it was the unity of people who commonly cared for the deceased and for the surviving family or friends that was center stage. The final departure from this life of one human being brought together many others to help each other cope with the loss. As sad as the loss of the deceased was, the event triggered strong associations of mutual caring, sharing, and hope.

The athletic team experience is somewhat similar in developing close spiritual bonds. Sports teams provide extensive missions and meaning to youth. There is always a mission of individual or team improvement, whether it involves developing better physical skills or mental abilities. There is always the next play, next at-bat, the next quarter or inning of play, or the next season. Sports unify team members and constantly provide some on-task future goal. In addition to mutual sharing in celebrations of victories, team members share losses and hard times together. Through associations and mutual support in the pursuit of a common mission, youth are provided a sense of added meaning. Their actions affect more than just themselves; the lives of others, their teammates, are also affected.

Teen gangs also provide mutual support of a different kind, a support for which our society pays a heavy price, as indicated by the letter from New York State Senator Alton R. Waldon, Jr., quoted in chapter 1. In addition to providing security and emotional support, as described in the first chapter, teen gangs are often the only viable source of meaning and hope that these youth perceive as being available to them. The gang provides youth with a feeling of being wanted and valued, which ignites and fuels hope and a sense of empowerment. School sports do the same thing. But sports and other co-curricula provide youth with a strong but positive alternative model of this sense of hope and empowerment.

Flexible Planning & Setting Direction

This area of concern is very important in adapting to change, since it is the process by which our lives are continuously "invaded by the future," as phrased by Alvin Toffler. Renewing companies always keep an eye to the future, via the planning process; yet, they keep the plans flexible, as circumstances take their capricious turns. All the while, such companies remain optimistic in their pursuit of their ultimate goals: profitable results from continued improved service to customers, and staying ahead of competition.

Waterman (1988, 30) presents a vivid metaphorical illustration of how, in renewing companies, flexible planning operates so effectively in absorbing and working through stochastic shocks of the business world by quoting a portion of an essay by Herbert Simon, "The Psychology of Thinking." Much as the ant makes its way across the sands of an ocean beach on a windy day, flexible planning as experienced in school sports and other co-curricular programs can be helpful to individuals, as well as renewing companies:

> Thus (the ant) makes his weaving, halting way back to his home. So as not to anthropomorphize about his purposes, I sketch the path on piece of paper. It is a sequence of irregular, angular segments - not

quite a random walk, for it has an underlying sense of direction, of aiming toward a goal...Viewed as a geometric figure, the ant's path is irregular, complex, hard to describe. But its complexity is really a complexity in the surface of the beach, not a complexity of the ant.

Simon's metaphor represents a very close likeness to the unpredictable forces in the business world, as well as to the dance of life in general. We have to keep moving forward. Yet in our efforts to do so, we are often forced to adjust our long range plans by unforseen changes which life throws at us.

Similarly, school sports provide a living metaphor of the changeable dance of life. Other than sports, few activities can simulate the ongoing changes characteristic of the dance of life. Unexpected change is as common in sports programs as it is in business, if not more so. When the football star receiver drops the pass on a critical fourth down play in a tied game; when the defensive team lines up in a formation that the offensive team has never seen before; when the all-star baseball outfielder drops the flyball, or the pitcher throws a wild pitch to score the tying run in the bottom of the ninth inning; when the basketball star misjudges where to throw a pass and the ball goes out of bounds in the final seconds of a tied game; when the weather conditions change giving the other team an advantage because of their style of play; when the injuries to the first and second team players at a particular position forcing a reserve player with no prior game experience to play in a big game; when your football team is on its own five yard line with a one point lead, with a fourth down and 25 yards to go for a first down in the last few seconds of the game and the only player on your team who can punt lines up in your end zone with a broken hand to handle the ball; these and all subsequent last minute changes of a team's strategy result from unexpected change. Student-participants are constantly presented opportunities to experience and adapt to stochastic changes such as these.

The examples of unpredictable occurrences in sport and the efforts of participants to effectively respond to them are endless. They commonly mirror the dance of life to which we all must adapt. They provide a testing ground by which youth can practice skills which are transferrable to life's real game, outside of the sports arena. Just like the ant on the windy beach in Herbert Simon's metaphor, sports participants must make constant adjustments to continually occurring changes in their environment as they pursue their general goal of winning the game. School sports help students realize the importance of having a general direction and a flexible plan whether in games or in life.

Stability In Motion

This characteristic is strongly connected to flexible planning, as discussed above. Renewing business organizations not only accept the fact that change is inevitable; their leaders often anticipate and welcome change as normal. These leaders breed stability among the people of their organizations by promoting the idea that change is a normal occurrence. They do not set plans with expectations that there will be little or no change occurring.

On the contrary, renewing companies design plans in conformity with the organization's mission. But, the plans are also developed with the expectation that unknown changes will inevitably take place. Changes are viewed, not with a complacent attitude, but are accepted as the norm and anticipated as possible opportunities. This opportunistic attitude about change is reminiscent of Alexis de Tocqueville's observations of how Americans, during the early 1800's, welcomed change and adapted to its insidious and often difficult surprises.

A French political theorist, de Tocqueville travelled to America over 160 years ago to study our prison system. In the nine months that he spent here, however, he became more interested in the American culture, the ways of life of the American people. He consequently spent most of his time studying Americans, how they lived, and how they went about practicing their democratic principles. In his 1832 essay, "The Restless American Spirit," de Toqueville describes how Americans related to change:

> ...Often born under another sky, placed in the middle of an ever moving picture, driven himself by the irresistible torrent that carries all around him along, the American has no time to attach himself to anything. He is only accustomed to change and ends by looking on it as the natural state of man. Much more, he feels the need of it, he loves it. For instability, instead of causing disasters for him, seems only to bring forth wonders around him. The idea of a possible improvement, of a successive and continuous better ment of the social condition, that idea is ever before him in all its facets (Mayer, 1971).

The knowledge that unknown changes will occur at unpredictable times is central to efforts by the renewing companies to establish a strong and worthwhile mission. A clearly defined mission statement helps all of the members of the organization stay focused on the "big picture" when those inevitable changes strike. School sports also have an agenda, which includes winning games against an opponent. Their overall mission, however, is for team members to pursue improvement of themselves, as well as their teammates, individually and collectively. Consistent effort in practice and games is the precursor to individual and team improvement. Like sports, improvement in life is not achieved in large, dramatic ways. It usually comes about in very small steps. It is a daily process of improving by inches, instead of by feet or yards.

Waterman notes (245) that renewing business organizations tend to encourage continuous changes by aiming for small wins on a regular basis rather than always seeking huge victories or "quantum leap" wins. Although games can be won by large scores, the efforts of players in the actual games are a very small percentage of an athlete's development. Most of his or her improvement results from the many repeated efforts in team and individual training. The same is true, of course, for people in business and life in general. How many times do doctors, lawyers, carpenters, clerks or secretaries have to repeat the skills of their trade, in various circumstances, before they become consistently proficient in their work?

Sports teams, renewing companies, and other successful organizations remain stable by accepting and challenging changes, regularly, in small, incremental steps. Sports activities present conditions which force participants to adapt to stochastic changes and measure one's performance against his own prior efforts and that of others. As a result, another important benefit of school sports is the daily opportunity for youth to face and overcome the challenges and adversities prompted by stochastic change. Through opportunities to experience improvement in small and regular steps, youth can develop habits characteristic of individuals and organizations who regularly and successfully adapt to stochastic life changes.

Persistence

According to Waterman, renewing companies consider each employee an important part of the organization's success, and they communicate that perspective throughout the firm. Each employee is viewed as an asset who is a "source of creative input." Likewise, school sports and other co-curricular programs provide youth with constant opportunities for the realization of his or her potential while also making an impact on his or her team. While learning that he can make a difference in the lives of his or her teammates either in practice and/or games, he experiences the ability to influence events. Even when results are disappointing, a participant who persists in times of adversity still has the opportunity to gain respect for himself and from his teammates. One of the most difficult challenges for everyone is to persist through disappointing situations. This can also be one of the greatest sources for empowerment.

Bob Shannon, the highly successful football coach at East St. Louis High School (Illinois) for the past seventeen years, claimed that the challenge of disappointment is one of the most empowering of student-athletic experiences. "Even when players fail in an attempt to do something or if they are not on the first team, they still earn respect of others as well as themselves by passing the test of hanging in when challenged, by persisting through adversity" (Shannon, 1992). That is a particularly meaningful testimony coming from a youth mentor whose high school is located in one of America's most economically deprived areas yet who still turns out championship teams of players who also perform well in the classroom.

Continual Measurement of Performance

Renewing companies have a penchant for numbers, statistics, and facts. These firms use such information as a "scoreboard," with which to make internal comparisons of their current performance levels against prior work. Of course, numbers, in the form of dollars and units of merchandise produced and sold, are the primary means used to measure their performance against that of their competitors. Like the renewing companies, keeping such data in school sports programs provide an objective yardstick to analyze effort and minimizes subjectivity in evaluation of performance. It provides student-participants modeling and actual experience in making personal progress by measured improvements.

Commitment

Teamwork involves commitment of team members to the task of mutual support for their improvement as a unit and individually. Webster's defines teamwork as "The quality whereby individuals unselfishly subordinate their own part to the general effort of the group with whom they are working or playing." Yet, even though individual members put the team's overall goal above their own concerns, they benefit individually: the same symbiotic principle of individual citizen's rights within the overarching needs of the community which is the underpinning of our Constitution. Both trust and commitment are fundamental to the fabric of our Constitution as well as to that of a team.

Commitment is a strong word. It means that you mean what you say and you will follow through on your promises. It is an old word with important contemporary connotations. Within it is contained the lifeblood of civilization. Where commitment is tenuous at best, or where it has lost meaning altogether, therein lie the seeds of dissolution of relationships and, ultimately, society. Unless I can count on the word of another that he will follow through on his stated commitment, I am limited in my own capacity to make a commitment, either to myself or to others. Society involves an ongoing myriad of commitments, both small and large, as we try to anticipate future actions required of us.

Commitment is embodied, as well as constantly practiced during participation in school sports as well as other co-curricular activities. Of particular significance regarding commitments practiced in co-curricular activities is that they are made voluntarily by student-participants. Exercising one's choice, participation, and voluntary commitments are central to a democratic society, particularly the United States.

Trust

Commitment begins with trust: the cornerstone of human relationships. When I trust another, it means I can count on him or her. It is fundamental to individual relationships as well as those involving groups of people. In fact, Robert Waterman reports that "trust" was an essential ingredient in successful efforts of renewing companies.

Trust is particularly important in the foundation and operation of democratic society. Citizens of a democracy place their trust in elected offi-

cials to act on behalf of the common good, above any official's interests.
The election process is based on the issue of trust.

Unfortunately, the trust factor is being eroded in our culture. Let us
further consider the important place trust has in our individual and collective lives, how it is being eroded in our country, and the value of school
sports in helping youth to experience trust through commitment to a team
of others as well as oneself.

In our discussion of "anomie" in chapter 2, we addressed the precarious conditions regarding millions of our nation's youth. Mixed messages
have increasingly become a catalyst for confusion and mistrust in the
development of our youth. Particularly for the millions of young people
living with only one, or neither, of their natural parents, and whose primary model of any type of direction are other wayward youth, trust is a
difficult concept to know.

Increased exposure by media of improprieties and inconsistencies by
contemporary political figures further erodes the trust factor in our culture, not only for youth, but for those of all ages. The inability of the
United States Congress to balance the federal budget during the 1980's
and '90's, one of its primary duties, is one example. Another example is
the recent expose of the practice, by scores of Congressional representatives of consistently writing checks on bank accounts having insufficient
funds. Recent public opinion polls are revealing voters' unparalleled dis-
may with politicians' misuse of the trust which people have confided in
them.

Although the Constitution is the bedrock of our republic, *The Federalist Papers* are generally recognized as the most authoritative analysis
and explanation of this great document. This collection of essays was
written separately by three of America's most influential founding fathers: Alexander Hamilton, John Jay, and James Madison. The word
"trust," although implied in both the Declaration of Independence as well
as the Constitution, is not specifically stated in either document. However, according to James Madison, referred to as the Father of the Constitution, clarifies, the idea of trust was central in our nation's inception and
the development of our fundamental laws. In his essay Number 46 of the
Federalist Papers, Madison declares that the role of government is to be
"trustee" of the people: The federal and State governments are, in fact,
but different agents and trustees of the people, constituted with different
powers and designated for different purposes.

In essay Number 57, Madison asserts that primary goals of any political constitution should be twofold: (1) to acquire governmental representatives who will pursue the common good of those they represent, and (2) to provide the means to hold those representatives in their efforts on behalf of the people to maintain the public "trust" in them.

Trust: absolutely fundamental for healthy relationships and the conduct of a government's responsibility to the people it serves. It is an important trait that is regularly encouraged and practiced in school sports and other co-curricular programs.

Team

Although people have always combined their efforts through some type of teamwork when performing heavy tasks, contemporary business organizations have increasingly stressed the formal concept of "team" in their operations. The team concept is particularly characteristic of the renewing companies, according to Waterman. These renewing companies not only find that more quality work is accomplished via teamwork, but teams of talented people also generally respond more effectively to the stochastic changes which are so inherent in the workplace.

Charles Garfield (1986, 173) describes how, from the time the earliest settlers landed on American shores, the combination of individual effort and collaboration with others was more the rule than the exception in American history. Whether it was early settlement of the eastern seaboard or movement of pioneers westward, team work was a prime factor in basic survival as well as small and great achievements. The managers who attempt to motivate their employees and operate their businesses on the principle of intimidation still exist. According to Garfield (179), however,

> ...among our peak performers we see far more recognition of the motivational power of teamwork through alignment - alignment based on both the enlightened self-interest of an individual and the best interests of an organization.

Alignment clarifies the relationship between the members of a team. Although they may have various differences of opinion regarding how a task should be completed, their ultimate mission is to succeed, to get the job done. As noted earlier in this chapter, Robert Waterman observed that a common cause or mission spawns commitment of team members to pursue the achievement of that mission for themselves and for each other. Garfield (1986, 89) uses a sports metaphor to clarify the process and value of alignment in this context:

> An easy way to understand this kind of alignment is to look at an athlete's effort and contribution to a team. For both individual and organization, the mission may be the same: to be the best. The individual wants the team to succeed because it provides the context for his or her own personal achievement. Obviously, the presence of such committed individuals improves the odds that the organization will succeed...

One of the greatest testimonies to the experience of being a part of a team was heard by millions across the nation and around the world on Sunday, February 16, 1992. On this significant day in the history of basketball, the formal, albeit premature, retirement ceremony for Erwin "Magic" Johnson was nationally televised. Emotions ran deep during the affair, as Magic's family sat nearby him while holding back tears. Several noteworthy professional basketball personalities such as Kareem Abdul-Jabar, Larry Bird, and Jerry West lauded Magic for all he had done for basketball, as well as various charitable organizations.

Following the other speakers, Magic stepped up to the podium, where he graciously acknowledged the tributes and tumultuous applause from the thousands in attendance. As his own occasional tears broke through his efforts to hold them back, he spoke of the many valuable experiences he has had in the course of his playing days. He noted various opportunities afforded him as a result of basketball, and the many awards and honors for which he was grateful. However, the most touching moment of his speech was when he announced that the experience he missed above all others, now that he was no longer playing, is that of simply being "one of the boys" on the team. Above all, he missed being part of the team family, the fraternity of guys who helped each other get better in basketball but who cared for each other beyond the sport itself. He missed the daily renewal of the bonding experience of the "team."

While listening to Magic describe how the team itself was the most important aspect of his involvement in sports, I was reminded of how that was also true for me. And, during the years I coached on the high school and college levels, it was apparent that most of the players with whom I had the opportunity to work evidenced this same sentiment. All of those with whom I consulted regarding this book emphasized that bonding, being a part of a team and forming strong relationships with others, was one of the most beneficial experiences they observed in students who participated in school sports and other co-curricular activities. They commented how such relationships positively affect self-esteem, as student-participants experienced others caring for them. Participants develop a sense of belonging which is so important to adolescents. Such students also feel good about contributing to the good of their fellow participants. One of these consultants, Dr. Roberto Perez (1992), Vice Principal at Willow Glen High School in San Jose, California, told me:

> ..school sports kept me from dropping out of high school. In school sports I developed important bonds with other guys on the team that helped me get through difficult times. Bonding with others in a meaningful and constructive activity is probably the most important experience of school sports for youth, as far as I am concerned!

As schools are charged with educating our youth, they must do so within an environment of constant change. The task is made ever more difficult by the daunting sense of rootlessness and weakening of values that are outgrowths of widespread dissolution of families and pervasive dispersion of mixed messages. An important means by which we can empower schools to help students become empowered to overcome these and other social order disturbances is to provide the funds necessary to conduct extensive co-curricula programs with full time teacher mentors. School co-curricular activities will provide students constructive educational alternatives, in which they can voluntarily experience the bonding experience they need and otherwise seek in gangs and other perilous involvements.

Chapter 5

Hope & Empowerment

It's an open secret that sport is a chance for children from orphanages to succeed in the world. - Olympic bicycle sprint champion Erika Salumae of the Soviet Union

As I noted earlier, youth are seeing more hope in the support gained from the affiliation of gang membership, in pursuing crime activities which result in immediate gratification of their needs and desires. It is difficult for them to have any hopeful aspirations beyond the moment. Forget about delayed gratification that comes from hard work and sacrifice over time. Denied the modeling of these principles by significant mentors, and lacking a sense of security and roots of a supportive family, youth tend to imitate the apparently successful actions which bring the only observable and understandable hope they see: get whatever-you-can, however-you-can, now!

Hope is particularly important in our consideration of the value of school sports and other co-curricular programs for two reasons: (1) hope is essential to sustain health and even life itself while overcoming adversities in the dance of life, and (2) school sports provide both a strong model of hope and effective means for youth to personally experience hope: the belief that we have another chance!

Hope: Having Another Chance

The psychological state of depression is not the opposite of hope. Death is. Lost hope is a powerful ally of decay, of illness. On the other hand, where a flame of hope continues to burn, individually or collectively, even if it is a small flicker, detrimental circumstances cannot completely destroy potential for renewal. As long as there is even a small sense of hope, the effects of defeat and feelings of helplessness are held at bay.

A vibrant life is synonymous with hope. Hope is believing that something good can happen, that one has something to look forward to. Hope is the belief that one has a chance to have a better tomorrow than today or that he or she will be better tomorrow than he is today. It is particularly strong when a person believes that he or she has the capability to effect positive changes in his or her life.

Of all the positive effects of sports activities, none is more important than their constant reminder and reinforcement of hope. Sports always provide us with another chance for a better tomorrow. Whether we win or lose today, whether we have a winning or losing season, we have the next game or the next season to look forward to; a season in which we can aspire to become better than our previous record of achievement. Sports contests regularly present us with a metaphor of hopeful striving in which we can reach beyond the successes or the obstacles of the present moment and experience better moments of the future.

Before we look at the specific ways in which school sports and other co-curricular activities promote a sense of hope among student-participants, let us first consider the importance of hope to our individual lives and our nation in general.

The Importance of Hope in Our Lives

We all look forward to having the possibility of a better tomorrow: this is the essence of hope.

Hope is important to health and achievement. It opens doors in our thinking, prompts positive biochemical reactions inside our bodies, and promotes enhanced relationships with others. In addition, hope is the ultimate promise of our United States Declaration of Independence and Constitution. Both of these documents embody hope for self-determination and the democratic principle.

Scores of medical and other scientific studies over the past 30 years have demonstrated the strong links between hope and health, both physical and mental, as well as various human achievements. Among the most classic accounts of the importance of hope to human existence are those of war-time prison camp survivors. Survivors of the World War II Nazi death camps and prisons of various other wars attest to hope reigning at the top among factors enabling them to continue their efforts to live.

In a recent newspaper article entitled, "Hope Emerges as the Key to

Success in Life," Dr. Daniel Goleman (1992) briefly summarizes the numerous findings of research which verify the critical effects of hope in human living:

> Psychologists are finding that hope plays a surprisingly potent role in giving people a measurable advantage in realms as diverse as academic achievement, bearing up in onerous jobs, and coping with tragic illness. And, by contrast, the loss of hope is turning out to be a stronger sign that a person may commit suicide than other factors long thought to be more likely risks...

Research findings from a recent study, cited by Goleman, which was conducted by Dr. Charles Snyder, University of Kansas psychologist, specifically demonstrate the effects of hope on the academic performance of college freshman. Results showed that the level of hope of first-year students at the beginning of their initial semester proved to be a more accurate predictor of academic success than either their SAT scores or their high school grade point average.

Noteworthy books which summarize a considerable amount of significant research findings referred to by Goleman are listed under references (Cousins, 1979; Seligman, 1975, 1990; Dubos, 1978).

Goleman's observations, and those of Victor Frankl, Martin Seligman, and Albert Bandura (discussed at the beginning of chapter 4) imply strongly that hopeful anticipation relates positively with continued efforts to adapt. Also, these observations strongly suggest the efficacy of proactive and constructive activities, such as are involved in school sports and other co-curricula, to instill hope and empower youth for positive ends.

Youth on the Edge

In addition to the millions of children and adolescents living in socially troubled conditions today, there are many others who live on the edge: those who would not be numbered among the economically deprived which is typically associated with those who live in poor and run down areas. Yet, while attending schools relatively free of the violence plaguing inner-city schools, these students face the ravages of broken homes, alcoholic parents, and/or parents who constantly argue or even physically fight. I know this situation all too well, as I was an only child in such a home. My story is tame compared to others, but it involves reflections of the deep sadness, frustrations, and anger that children of such homes carry with them while growing up as well as later in life; it enables me to easily relate to them.

I was fortunate not to be raised in a slum area. My neighborhood was lower-middle-class with small, 700 square-foot houses built as part of a post World War II housing development. I knew that my parents loved me. I never had to want for food or other basics in the way of clothing and shelter. My parents' incomes were modest, but they insisted that I attend Catholic elementary school and high school because they thought the discipline was more strict than in public schools. So, while we did not have many extras in the way of worldly goods, I lived comfortably - except for the insecurity of not knowing when fights would break out between my parents.

My parents' alcoholic and marital problems seemed relatively minimal when I was very young. But during my junior high school years, their heavy drinking and fighting episodes steadily increased. Two weekends each month were consumed by loud verbal fights, and an occasional hole would be smashed in a wall or window by a fist or some thrown object.

In addition to worrying about my parents' safety, particularly my mother's, as my dad would sometimes lose his senses, I felt very embarrassed. More often than not, neighbors would hear the noise coming from the house late at night or in the early morning hours - when these disputes flared up. I remember all too well the fear I would have that my parents would come home drunk. Would they argue and start the loud yelling? Would the yelling lead to some physical violence? I thought of myself then as a kid who the neighbors saw as being tainted. I was always embarrassed by the physical appearance of my house, as the years wore on and these violent alcoholic incidents increased. It was particularly sad for me to have to physically restrain my dad from going after my mother or from taking some other action that might have harmed him. I remember how much I frequently regretted even living.

I had very low self-esteem, which was due a great deal to the constant embarrassment I felt. But it sometimes helped to consider that there were many others who had it far worse than I did. Although that was, in fact, the truth, I don't remember knowing any other kids who experienced the same fears and embarrassment at that time. Of course, over the years since my freshman year in college, when I first lived away from home, I have become acutely aware of how many millions of other young people had it worse than I did.

Did this have any negative bearing on my academic performance? Very much so. Frequent feelings of frustration and depression lowered my motivation to study on numerous occasions. I often just worried a great deal about my home situation, which naturally interfered with my ability to focus on study assignments.

I was also fortunate, as I mentioned, in that I knew my parents loved me. In addition, my dad did not drink for the last 8 years of his life before he died of a heart attack at age 54. I really only got to know him the last couple years of his life. In spite of my own struggle with the anxieties, anger, frustrations, and sadness of my growing years, I was fortunate to have had a sense of hope, belonging and a source of at least a measure of self-esteem, albeit at a low level. I attended schools in which student unrest and antisocial behaviors were practically non-existent. And, my parents completely encouraged my participation in sports, which were strongly supported at my elementary and high schools.

Just like children and adolescents growing up in all areas of the country, I gravitated to close associations with other youth. My best friends were my chief sources of support and direction, except for my athletic coaches. I can still remember the special feeling of value I received from my junior high school coaches. In particular, I recall the very important feeling of support, encouragement, and care communicated by my high school coaches, Wally Moore and Gene Knutson. I am forever grateful to Coaches Moore and Knutson for the personal interest they invested in me during those critical years. They exemplify the empowering effects of concerned mentors, discussed both by Tracy Robinson of the L.A. City Attorney's Office relative to youth gangs and Nel Noddings, Associate Dean of Stanford University's School of Education, regarding the importance of caring and continuity in education.

For one thing, these coaches spent 2-3 hours with me every day during the season of a sport and often as much time in the off-season. There were many opportunities to provide encouraging words, or those of warranted criticism, as prompted by a careless or less-than-desirable action on my part, whether on or off the playing fields. They were also quick to express concern for my academic efforts if there was any concern that grades were not at the level they should be. The fact that an older person expressed sincere concern at all was empowering to me! Then, having those older people express their interest both on and off the field was additional proof that someone cared. Someone gave a damn! Someone who was involved with me during times involving demanding physical effort, encouraging, prodding, helping, motivating, sometimes yelling, other times softly encouraging, was also there with words of concern for me in other areas of my life. Their efforts had an empowering effect on me while I was developing in school, and were an important contribution to my life in general.

I was lucky to have friends from more stable homes who generally had positive direction, a sense of values, and common interests, especially in sports participation. We always had a focus on a positive activity or interest. Playing sports was not our only concern, but it was a focus that encouraged personal and team development even when we were not in school, studying at home, dating, or involved in some other activity.

When I think of the sad and depressing experiences I had when growing up in a turbulent home situation, I have greater empathy and concern for youth in our country who live (often barely) through much worse situations at home and/or in their neighborhood environments. I am also even more aware of the millions who live "on the edge" who could easily become involved with the deviant influences that offer affiliation and hope beyond that available to them in their daily environment. I was one of the fortunate young people who had friends with a positive direction and encouragement to participate in activities which provided structure and opportunity: to set goals, compete, receive support when down or defeated, and feel empowered by the physical development; receive acknowledgment from teammates and others, including teachers and parents, for successful efforts, and to gain a sense of direction which came from having goals, a plan to accomplish them, and a direction to pursue toward that end.

But, as a result of my experiences in school sports participation and the friends and other associations which resulted, the most prevalent emotion that I had was hope. Exposure to forward-thinking people who were interested in me as an individual and as a team member was a bonding experience that carried over into other areas of my life, and was instrumental in my never losing hope. But, in the momentary occasions when hope seemed to falter, I did not have time to think about that negative prospect. I had to go to practice! If I had a good practice, hopeful feelings re-emerged in the course of working at that on-task experience. If things did not go so well at practice, usually I had a buddy or two who would be there to "pick me up" or a coach to encourage me. Nothing short of a successful effort would return the feeling of hope that I felt when the teammate or coach was there to pick me up when I felt down.

All the while, I was involved in an on-task activity in cooperation with teammates, trying to help others, being helped myself, and bonding. And, I was usually painfully aware if I had not given a good effort. That was often the reason for a practice not going well for me. It usually proved to be a challenging lesson about the one thing over which I have control: my own thinking and effort.

Bonding & Hope

I found my own experience in forming lasting and positive influential bonds during my participation in school sports to be echoed throughout my interviews with the professionals I consulted for this work. As an example, the first reaction of Dr. Roberto Perez (1992) while we were discussing his experiences was that school sports kept him from dropping out of high school. Although he noted several positive effects of his participation in sports, the most important was the bonding effect of sports. Similar to Magic Johnson's words noted at the end of the last chapter, Perez claims that the close friendships he formed with other student-athletes had a very profound impact on him in overcoming negative temptations and to pursuing positive activities.

In agreement with Perez, Tracy Robinson suggests that the bonding experience in school sports and other co-curricular programs is significant in retarding the involvement of participants in youth gangs. The enthusiasm and support student-participants receive from teammates and coaches is very similar to bonds formed by members of a gang - often lacking in many homes. It's empowering to feel the support of teammates when you win and, particularly, in defeat (Robinson, 1992).

Robinson (1992) notes that school sports participation and the assistance he received from his coaches were important to his own development during junior and senior high school. He feels that one of the most valuable aspects which school sports provides is an opportunity for student-athletes to develop a mentoring relationship with his or her coach:

> During junior high school and early senior high school years, adolescents tend to be more open to a mentor's influence than in later years.

School sports provide a young person the opportunity for mentoring from an older and experienced and, hopefully, professionally trained educator.

Again, Tracy Robinson agrees with Stanford's Nel Noddings who claims that another of the advantages a coach has in mentoring youth, apart from being strongly involved with the student in mental and physical work, is continuity. Because a student-athlete spends extensive time each day and over a number of years with his or her coach, school sports participation allows for a more trusting and advisorial relationship (Noddings, 1992).

Another area of hope facilitated by sports participation is that of interracial and intercultural involvement. As our population grows increasingly diverse culturally today, we need activities to prompt common involvement among different people more than at any time in United States history. Not only were co-curricular activities originally developed in our public school system to help discourage gang membership and other youth-related problems at the turn of the twentieth century, they were also intended to help resolve cultural differences as the immigrant population grew dramatically in the late 1800's. Before we can expect people of different backgrounds to coalesce into agreeable relationships, we need to provide activities for their interaction on a "level playing field." No other single type of activity provides this occasion as equally as voluntary sports participation.

Frequent Modeling of Another Chance: New Hope

In addition to facilitating bonding as a source of hope, sports provide opportunities to have another chance in the face of temporary failures, and to look forward to new possibilities for self-improvement and a better tomorrow.

As discussed in chapter 3, most advancements are not made in quantum leaps. They are usually made intermittently, and not necessarily on a daily basis. When we make improvements in our observable performances or within ourselves at work or play, we do so amidst trials and errors; and our failed attempts usually outnumber our small successes, particularly early in our efforts to achieve a desired outcome. Most human growing experiences including those derived from formal, institutionalized activities of education and socialization are analogous to the process of a child goes through in first learning to ride a bicycle.

In the beginning, the child has to be completely aided by mom or dad. After several such assisted rides, the parent lets go of the bike while running alongside, letting the child pedal a short distance without aid. Eventually, the child must try it alone with the invariable spills. But, he or she strives toward the only vision he or she has: that of riding the bike. Eventually, through the trial and error process, the errors become fewer and the number of successful attempts increases, until the task is finally mastered. In our daily confrontations with stochastic changes, we similarly risk falling short of completing a task or overcoming a problem. We can feel empowered to keep trying, though, when we see examples of others who do so in the face of difficult challenges and defeats.

Sports provide us a living metaphor of the trial-and-error process that is involved in coping, improving, and renewing. In baseball, we step to the plate, swing at a pitch, and miss. Strike. We failed, right? No! We have another chance; we have two more strikes left, two more chances to succeed! But, we miss the next pitch! Strike two...still no failure; we have strike three. We have the next at-bat, the next inning, the next game, the next season.

And so it is in every sport. We always have the next attempt, the next game to look towards. Sports participation necessitates goal setting and goal-striving. As a result, participation prompts forward momentum in our thinking.

Falling short of points on the scoreboard in any one game, or even in any one entire season, does not mean final defeat. We can be hopeful because we can look to the next opportunity. Sports participation always holds out hope to improve ourselves, and our team, so that tomorrow can be a better day...and we can be better!

Hope is also fostered by providing an easily-observed means of self-comparison for self-improvement. Since the adoption of standards of measure from their evolution and application in manufacturing during the industrial revolution, sports records always stand as simple reference points to measure our individual or collective progress.

The implicit message of perpetual hope provided by sports participation is embodied in the inspiring song, "One Moment In Time," popularized by singer Whitney Houston. The message integrates all the hopeful efforts I have observed or read about in others who relentlessly pursued attainment of difficult goals in various life circumstances. It reflects the seed of hope ingrained in the statement of Erika Salumae at the beginning of this chapter, regarding sports and hope for orphans. It also typifies the vision of greater possibilities to those who have overcome personal tragedies through perseverance fueled by hope. In addition, the singer of this song admits that although she is only one, she is not alone - the essence of team bonding. Haven't we all experienced hope at one or several times for a better day or a better self and then struggled to achieve it as expressed by this song?

First stanza:

Each day I live,
I want it to be
A day to give, the best of me
I'm only one, but not alone
My finest day, is yet unknown
I broke my heart, for every gain
To taste the sweet, I faced the pain
I rise and fall, yet through it all
This much remains,
Refrain:
I want one moment in time, when I'm more
Than I thought I could be,
When all of my dreams are a heartbeat away
And the answers are all up to me,
Give me one moment in time, when I'm racing
With destiny,
Then in that one moment in time I will feel,
I will feel eternity...

While the song describes only one moment, don't we really have in our lives many moments, perhaps ongoing moments, that we hope to be better than we were in the past...a continuous striving to have better tomorrows than our yesterdays and todays?

Those who have ever identified a particular goal, whether in sports, academics, personal business pursuits, or any other activity, and followed an intended course of action involving sacrifice, discomfort, and perseverance through all types of obstacles, can probably relate at least several hopeful situations to the second stanza of the song:

I've lived to be the very best
I want it all, no time for less
I've laid the plans, now lay the chance
Here in my hands

Refrain:...

"One Moment In Time" beautifully embodies those quick hitting lightning bolts of the desire to be better than we are now. It talks of possibilities of being better, but implies the price required in hard work and struggle to achieve it. It challenges us to choose to strive to get better or to let the opportunity slip by. The song is a reflection of our desires for success, and also a reminder of the price we are required to pay for most achievements. It personifies the internal quest and related demands for success in sports, as well as our successes in overcoming difficult life circumstances in general, and, in particular, self-imposed obstacles.

Combining Sports with Academics and the "Field of Life"

The message of hopeful striving resounding in "One Moment In Time" is pursued weekly by the kids who participate in the Biddy Basketball League conducted by the Children's Aid Society in New York City. It is an excellent example of how hope can be successfully instilled by combining after-school sports with academics. It is a program run for youth between ages of 7-13, most of whom are being raised by single mothers on welfare. The program is conducted at the Frederick Douglass housing project in Upper West Side of Manhattan.

Begun in 1972 to provide some place for kids to play basketball, the program has included academic tutoring over the past few years, which has proven to be very successful. Conducted in two parts on Saturdays, the program requires interested youth to actively participate in the morning tutoring sessions before they are allowed to play basketball in the afternoon. They must also show tutors their school report cards with passing grades before they are allowed to play.

In addition to receiving awards for their athletic participation, each of the 80 participants also receive an award for their academic efforts. Basketball initially attracts participation by these youth, but they then get involved in the academic activity. The participants develop an awareness of their ability to learn in the classroom and have an opportunity to play basketball. It is a marriage of two learning experiences in which seeds of hope can be planted and cultivated.

Indeed, this is similar to the marriage of required classroom study involved in the core curriculum and co-curricular activities that was first begun during the late 1890's in the New York City school system. The need for such unifying activities in education was affirmed in the "The Cardinal Principles of Secondary Education" report issued in 1918 by the Commission on the Reorganization of Secondary Education, and discussed earlier in chapter 3 of this book. After this report was published, co-curricular activities were expanded in public education.

Another example of a successful combination of youth participation in sports and classroom efforts occurs each year in East St. Louis, Illinois. Eugene Methvin (1991) describes the situation at East St. Louis High School, which is a story of empowerment and hope in less than hopeful conditions.

In East St. Louis, rampant socio-economic impoverishment reflects a pervasive sense of hopelessness. To illustrate the extent of crime and anti-social behavior in the community of East St. Louis, Methvin notes that the team frequently hears the exchange of gunfire involved in drug dealings taking place in the neighborhood surrounding the school's athletic fields. The general destitution of the area is further evidenced by the discovery at a morning practice of the dead body of a drug dealer on one of the football fields.

Bob Shannon, though, is an exceptional promoter of hope in East St. Louis. In 15 years, he has developed a commendable record of successful work with youth in the deprived surroundings of the community by combining school sports with classroom work. Bob is a teacher and the head coach of the football team at East St. Louis High School. It is admirable that in the past 12 years his teams have won 5 Illinois state high school football championships, an accomplishment of which he is justifiably proud. However, he claims that he is just as proud of another achievement: the academic success his players have earned in the classroom while their teams have been so successful on the playing field.

The successful academic records of Shannon's football player and the other athletes at East St. Louis High School reflect the testimonies of the other professional educators with whom I consulted for this book. The consensus of their observations, spanning an accumulated 300 years of experience as educators, is that student-participants in school sports, as well as all other co-curricular programs, generally demonstrate better classroom behavior and earn higher grades than non-participants. These extensive observations corroborate the research findings (described in chapter 1) about the correlation of co-curricular participation with favorable performance in academics and other school behaviors.

I asked Bob Shannon how he gets this difficult job done in spite of all the depraved conditions surrounding the school community. How does he motivate his student-athletes to achieve both athletically and academically? His answer reflected no magic. In fact, it was a rather unsurprising response. The student-athletes in his program generally succeed, he believes, because he requires of them strong discipline and ethical standards. He instills pride, personal commitment to team effort, a strong work ethic and good study habits, and other important values which his players adapt and practice on the "field of life" following graduation. And, his players can participate on the football team only if they abide by all the team rules and those of society. One of the principles he most strongly enforces is, "You cannot be a good player and a bad citizen (Shannon, 1992)."

Methvin's (1992) following observations summarize Shannon's outstanding success in helping youth from such impoverished conditions become empowered and develop hope through his involvement with them in school sports:

> Shannon estimates that 60 percent of his players come from single-parent homes, and 80 percent receive public assistance...[His] great achievement has been to take undisciplined youths with little hope and turn them into proud young men with a chance...[Shannon claims that] 'Our kids have to win more than just a football game. They have to win at the game of life... Life isn't always fair, but we can still expect excellence from ourselves.'

According to Methvin (1992), one of Shannon's former players who is now a college assistant football coach hits the proverbial nail on the head regarding the message that Bob Shannon so effectively communicates in his high school sports program: "He tells me not what I want to hear but what I need to hear."

Bob Shannon is to be congratulated and admired for the outstanding service he provides for youth, because it is also a great service for the community and country when youth are so positively directed. He does a magnificent job of combining co-curricula activities with those of the core curricula in facilitating empowerment where there is otherwise little to no hope for youth. Fortunately, it is a story that is replicated, in various ways, in thousands of other schools across America, by dedicated educator-mentors and coaches like Bob Shannon.

Unfortunately, over the past quarter-century, funds have been substantially decreased in support of co-curricular programs. Schools across the nation have had to either eliminate or decrease the quality of band, drama, and other valuable activities as well as various sports teams. For lack of funds, many public high schools in California have eliminated freshman sports teams. As a result, thousands of youth are denied opportunities to share in the worthwhile experiences of participation. The freshman year in high school is a critical year of transition in adolescence. Participation in co-curricular programs provide opportunities to form relationships that just don't happen otherwise, as well as being involved in constructive activities which help them to develop direction and time management, as submitted by educators with whom I consulted for this work.

As I pointed out in chapter 1, co-curricular mentors and coaches spend extensive amounts of time with their student-participants, which is good in that it facilitates continuity and stronger student-teacher relationships. However, these mentors should have professional educational requirements, as much as any classroom teacher. Such positions should be performed by full-time teaching professionals as much as possible. Unfortunately, too many full time teacher-coaches have had to be replaced by part-time paid, or unpaid, individuals who have full-time occupations in other fields in recent years.

One of the disadvantages in replacing full-time teacher-coaches with part-timers is the lost value of potential daily interactions between co-curricular mentors with other faculty members, all of whom could regularly consult each other regarding the academic status of student-participants. Also, even though there are good part-time, non-teacher mentors, the full-time teacher-mentor generally receives much more training in education and behavioral sciences. We lose that professional preparation if we have to rely extensively on non-teacher mentors and coaches in this valuable aspect of education. Again, we need adequate numbers of professionally-trained educators in the important instruction of co-curricular activities as much as we do in language arts, math, sciences, social studies, and any other subject included among the core curricula.

Testimony regarding the deleterious effects of eliminating school sports or other co-curricula, or of decreasing their quality, is provided by three journalists from the *Washington Post* who have spent considerable time in covering school sports, as described by Thomas Boswell (1992) of that newspaper.

According to Boswell (1992), in the wake of the April, 1992 Los Angeles riots, Michael Wilbon of *The Post* conducted interviews among government and education officials in L.A. about the relationship of organized school sports to youth-related social problems over the previous ten years. Many interviewees believed that the dramatic growth of youth gangs strongly correlate with the decrease in school sports programs. *Post* journalist Bill Brubaker reported that the same situation has developed in Washington, D.C.

Boswell himself covered school sports during the 1970's in the Washington, D.C. area. His observations (1992) of the correlation between decreased school sports programs and increased youth problems agree with Wilbon's and Brubaker's, and they are particularly pointed:

> To the degree that sports flourished in a school, order was maintained.
> To the degree that interest in sports died - and with the internal authority
> of coaches and athletes -schools invited every form of disorder.

Essential to renewal and life itself, hope looks to the future. A valuable metaphor of hope, adaptation to change, and renewal, school sports and other co-curricula promote and reinforce these attributes, as well as equality in support of the twofold principle of our Constitution: individual equality and freedoms within the overarching claims of the group, the community. School sports and all other co-curricular programs complement classroom curricula to provide activities of hope which help to empower individuals and facilitate unification of students from diverse backgrounds. As a result, these voluntary school programs promote the empowerment of community, as well as individuals, which is so vital to a democracy.

Erika Salumae's statement quoted at the beginning of this chapter is certainly true for children of orphanages. But her message also widely applies to millions of other youth as well. School sports and other co-curricular programs provide youth ongoing proactive opportunities to regularly observe and personally experience a model of hope: having new opportunities to improve oneself and/or one's circumstances and those of one's team...for renewal...having another chance!

Chapter 6

Community, Values & Vision as Promoted by Co-Curricular Participation

> ...empires of the future are empires of the mind. - Winston Churchill

> A great civilization is a drama lived in the minds of a people. It is a shared vision; it is shared norms, expectations, and purposes. - John W. Gardner, Former U. S. Secretary of Health, Education, and Welfare

Like all other forms of government, democracies don't last forever; at least that has been the case throughout history. And, while conflicts develop from time to time with a formidable foreign power, the greatest ongoing potential threat to democratic forms of government comes from within the nation, not from outside. Over two hundred years ago, James Madison warned us of the potential risk of internal division posed by factions otherwise known as special interest or splinter groups.

In essay No. 10 of *The Federalist Papers*, Madison described a faction as follows:

> ...a number of citizens, whether amounting to a majority or a minority of the whole, who are united and actuated by some common impulse of passion, or of interest, adverse to the rights of other citizens, or to the permanent and aggregate interest of the community.

It appears Madison's apprehension regarding the potential divisiveness of factions was not unwarranted. In addition to the increasing cultural pluralism taking place in our country, there has been extensive growth in the number of special interest groups as reflected in the proliferation of political action committees. In 1971 there were approximately 74 political action committees competing for congressional votes in our nation's capitol. In 1991, by contrast, there were 4,094 P.A.C.'s: a 5,432% increase in only 20 years!

Lobbying among representatives of different groups is an important privilege and integral part of our republican form of democracy. However, the dramatic increase in individual pressure groups and cultural pluralism prompts an even greater need for activities which bring people together in common like school sports and other co-curricular programs. And, the earlier in our citizens' lives that we can promote such community-building activities, the better chance we have to encourage dialogue among them leading to tolerance of differences.

In earlier chapters, much of our discussion focussed on the value of co-curricular experiences as constructive alternatives to gang involvements and other socially deviant behaviors among youth. We also identified how the combination of core curricular subjects with co-curricular activities benefits the overall socialization and education of our youth. We will now further explore the process by which school sports and other co-curricular activities help forge vital components of our Constitution for the continuance of our nation: simultaneous promotion of individual needs and achievement, as well as the interests of the community. To help us understand that process, we first will consider the role of vision in community development and how co-curricular programs contribute to such a vision.

Vision and Community

Vision is fundamental to the existence of community. A democratic community of people only succeed in their efforts to coexist to the extent that the group agrees on and holds a common vision of what the most important living principles are. Without such a common vision, a community lacks the important reference points by which they organize their system of government and rules of conduct. A common vision of values provides important guidelines for what or who citizens of a community wish to be. Such a vision also helps them stay on course, particularly during times that pose a strong challenge to their unity: times such as civil unrest, economic downturns, and differences between significant social and political factions.

When values are lacking or community members are confused as to what those values are, anomie (the state of normlessness discussed in chapter 1) and disharmony result. A business organization is a good example. In a business community, efficiency of operation, quality of products and services, and ultimately, profits, can suffer greatly from disharmony and disunity between labor and management as well as between the workers themselves. Over the past 15-20 years, decreased industrial productivity in the U.S. has often been attributed to our labor force having less regard for the age-old American hard-work and pride-in-quality ethic. Meanwhile, as we will discuss in more detail, the values of teamwork and harmonious enterprise of the Japanese in relation to their high rate of productivity are rapidly becoming legendary in management literature and among those who study business activities (Dourtouzos et al., 1989).

Organizations do not become institutions until they are infused with values. According to Tom Peters and Robert Waterman (1981) in *In Search of Excellence: Lessons from America's Best-Run Companies*, the best-run American companies did not achieve their tremendous success until after they had both established a clear vision of values and adopted those values throughout their organizations:

> Every excellent company we studied is clear on what it stands for, and takes the process of value shaping seriously. In fact, we wonder whether it is possible to be an excellent company without clarity of values... Virtually all of the better performing companies we looked at...had a well-defined set of guiding beliefs (281).

Significantly, the word "vision" was emphasized in a very meaningful and hopeful way by the MIT Commission on Industrial Productivity in their report (Dertouzos et al., 1989) of an extensive study of American manufacturing production deficiencies during the 1970's and '80s. Although the report points out basic weaknesses of American manufacturing organizations in general, the authors note that the investigators came away from the study with a positive perspective:

> ...there is certainly no cause for despair. In the course of its work, the Commission discovered many American firms that are thriving in the new economic climate and indeed are leading the way in international competition. The success of those firms suggest a vision of a new industrial America, a nation equipped to exploit the best ideas and innovations from abroad as well as its own inherent strengths (8).

The word "vision" pulls together the sense of optimistic perspective which comes to mind when we think of having hope; we can see the possibilities of a better tomorrow. When a group of people can commonly envision such hopeful possibilities, the probability that they will move in an intended direction or to accomplish a shared task is greatly enhanced.

But, how does this information relate to co-curricular activities, including school sports and community, in America? Everything.

No other single type of activity in our country so widely and clearly provides a vision of and reinforces our democratic ideals as that involved sports, particularly school sports. No other single type of activity presents and promotes a vision of the primary two-fold principle on which our Constitution is based: individual achievement and liberties are treasured, but only within the good of the community as regulated by popularly determined law. And, significantly, all such activities are entered upon by participants voluntarily; there are no mandates for participation. The vision that these activities facilitate is developed as a result of participants' choice, which is fundamental to democratic principles.

Values, Self-Improvement, Leisure & Sport in America

Since students are not required to participate in co-curricular programs, such programs are considered to be recreational, and are therefore conducted after required classroom hours. Similar to the situation of adults in which leisure time is considered to be non-work related, school programs that are not required fall into the same general category of activities. What place do these types of non-work-related, recreational, or leisure activities have among our American cultural values? How do such student activities affect the community of our nation? In the following sections, we will look at the answers to these questions and related issues.

As discussed earlier, Alexis de Tocqueville observed over 150 years ago that one of the most significant principles operating among people of the United States was that of democratic or individual achievement. That is, in America, people are allowed to improve themselves regardless of their family heritage. In our democracy, individuals can exercise their freedom of opportunity to better themselves regardless of family name, social or economic status, and without the strictures of the prescribed rules of a caste system. In America, more than almost anywhere else in the world, people have the freedom to improve themselves spiritually, educationally, financially, and physically.

This principle of self-improvement is strongly connected to America's nationwide participation in and love affair with sports. Dr. A. Bartlett

Giamatti, the late Commissioner of Major League Baseball, former President of Yale University, and eminent Renaissance scholar, gives us a hint as to the reason why.

In his book, *Take Time For Paradise*, Giamatti (1991) suggests that we can learn far more about a society by looking at its leisure and recreational activities than at those which are work-related. True, we can learn much about the technological development of a society by studying its work-related activities. However, it is during a person's leisure hours spent away from work, time spent away from required activities, that he or she is free to do whatever he or she chooses. And, when a person can freely choose to spend his non-imposed time, he or she usually engages in activities that reflect most accurately what is of greatest interest and value to him or her. That is, by examining a person's choice of activities to pursue during leisure time, we can know what he or she considers to be most important.

Giamatti notes that the word "recreation" was originally meant to describe an activity in which a person could recreate, or at least modify, some aspect of himself. Through recreation, then, a person would, in essence, improve himself spiritually, mentally, and/or physically. In this way, recreation was synonymous with "breathing new life" into a person during his free waking hours.

Dr. Giamatti further clarifies the connection between leisure activities and personal development by explaining the derivation of the word leisure itself. He points out that our English words "leisure" and "school" have the same derivation. Both words come from the Greek word "schole" which means to learn; i.e., through leisure activities, one learns, or has the opportunity to do so. While school is associated with learning in a formal context, leisure was meant to involve informal learning.

Leisure, then, was originally viewed as time for personal improvement and growth via informal learning and recreation of self.

Voluntary Co-curricular Programs: Their Value to Community

One of the great advantages of the recreational learning experiences afforded by co-curricular activities in school is that they are voluntary. Students freely choose to participate in them. Of course, students today are allowed a measure of choice regarding certain classroom courses. To fulfill academic requirements in certain subject areas, they are allowed to choose from among a select list of elective class offerings. However, there is still a difference of free choice between any classroom electives and co-curricular activities: students are required to participate in some classroom experiences of an elective, albeit one of their choice, whereas there is no requirement to participate in any co-curricular programs.

The fact that the co-curricular activities are completely voluntary is significant for many reasons. To begin with, our Constitution allows us to participate voluntarily in the experience of living in this country. Required classroom learning of core subject material is, of course, indispensable in our acquisition of information regarding historical facts, awareness of socio-economic and other issues of American and other societies, and quantitative and language skills. Such additional knowledge better equips us to understand and uphold the principles of the Constitution and, hopefully, to be much better prepared to elect capable leaders, as intended by the founding fathers. Not incidentally, concentrated study of core curricular material exercises higher-order thinking skills and provides information that can help prepare citizens for employment in America's work force.

But the great hope provided to us by our Constitution is that we can voluntarily exercise our individual freedoms to pursue the democratic achievement principle within the law. This hope is an integral part of the vision held out by the Constitution. Freely-chosen participation in co-curricular programs provides students with the opportunity to practice, voluntarily, interaction and self-initiative skills necessary to the individual and collective pursuit of that vision.

Ultimately, we voluntarily participate in a democratic form of government but are required to perform certain other actions also, such as work for our living. In this sense, an educational program incorporating the required curricula of the classroom with voluntary co-curricular activities benefits youth in two distinct ways: (a) it gives youth the opportunity to experience a model of the real world of required and voluntary activities, and (b) such a combined program lets youth extend their learning experience in the classroom to their freely-chosen leisure activities. In the process, students are presented yet another learning experience, as they are required both to balance time demands and schedule activities appropriately.

Co-curricula: Extended Classroom Learning Experiences

When speaking of the "classroom," we tend to think in terms of a room, located in a school building, in which students congregate to learn various subjects, as presented by a teacher via some structured lesson plan. Ara Parseghian, the very successful former head football coach at the University of Notre Dame offers an expanded view. He contends that the classroom is not limited to walls within a building.

According to Coach Parseghian, the classroom can be anywhere, at any time, because life itself is a learning process. As we discussed in chapter 3, life is a dance, involving our actions and reactions to stochastic changes. Within this extended context of education, Parseghian eloquently describes the educational value of athletic programs:

> I suppose it [has been] natural to place more intense emphasis on the teaching of core subjects [during the post-World War II nuclear age and the successful Russian space launch of Sputnik I, initiating the subsequent space race], but we seemed to forget parts of our history. We seemed to forget that man is a sum total of all his living experience which comes in many ways. We seemed to forget that the actual channels of learning differ with each student...and that each student will tend to stress those channels which give expression to his own best talents. The right of the individual to express and achieve according to his own talents and decisions seemed to get lost in our national effort to compete in space research.
>
> In this whole process, we tended to overlook the great distinction between knowledge and wisdom. We achieve wisdom only through living experience. The classroom can be anywhere, any time for anyone (Parseghian & Pagna, 1971, 297).

Parseghian did not consider himself as just a football coach. Instead, he saw himself as a "people coach," because he felt a responsibility to help his players learn from their athletic experience. He observed student-athletes develop several important values as a result of their participation in sports. He notes three in particular that he has observed student-athletes carry with them to the "classroom of life" following graduation:

> (1) the ability to reach out and "demand greater effort of himself," achieving much more than he previously believed he could and increasingly self-confidence as a result; (2) sacrifice, in which a student-athlete delays or gives up some other preferred action (or inaction, as the case may be) for the sake of another player or for the team; (3 the

ability to bounce back, to persist in times of difficulty and defeat, to keep
trying in spite of pain, pressure or sorrow...Loyalty...compassion...personal
pride ...enthusiasm...self-discipline...faith in one's self...surely these are
qualities worthy of respect. They are not acquired through merely reading; these are achieved through living (298)!

Dr. Nel Noddings, Associate Dean of Stanford University's School
of Education, offers valuable personal insight regarding motivational benefits of co-curricular activities to promote better performance in core curricular subjects. During the twenty years she taught high school math,
and in raising ten children of her own, she has seen how co-curricular
programs can act as bridges to interest students in core subjects in which
they initially had no interest or motivation to study (personal interview,
1992):

I believe that school sports and other co-curricular programs can
be implemented as even greater adjuncts to the overall learning experiences of students if faculty would do so. For instance, classroom conversations in literature, English, and social sciences could be based on
several different topics regarding sports or other co-curricular activities in which youth are interested and to which they can easily relate.
Examples of such topics might include the use of steroids in sports,
commercial advertisements involving sports issues or athletes, issues
related to particular other contests, etc.

Across the board, the educators with whom I consulted regarding
students' participation in co-curricular programs noted that during the
season of their sport or other activity, student participants usually earned
higher grades and manage their time better. They seem to participate in
the learning process more completely. Student participation in co-curricular program correlated with positive classroom behavior and performance, according to these educators.

Observations of several other educators, who agree with those of Dr.
Noddings regarding the educational value of co-curricular programs and
their potential to enhance the overall learning experience of youth, are
described in a special *San Jose Mercury News* article (Guersch, 1990),
"Sports Really Are Physical Education, Teachers Say." The high school
administrators and teachers cited in the article comment on their belief
that participation in school sports promotes self-esteem, bonding of relationships, and a positive attitude regarding school in general.

In particular, the Principal of Independence High School in San Jose, California, Dr. John Sallarole, makes the following claim:

> "...the best argument in favor of sports is that it bonds the kids to the school in a positive way. And if they feel good about the school, school will become a better experience for them!"

Beverly Lundstedt, mass media teacher at Independence High, agrees:

> Kids who become active in sports are generally better students because they know they can't sit around and do nothing in class... I have much better leverage on them than those who don't play, because my grade could make the difference on whether they play on the team... There are a lot of seniors in my class, and I've found out that a lot of them regret they didn't keep their GPA high enough to stay in sports. Many of them tell me that if they could go through high school again, they would have kept their GPA up and played sports (Guersch, 1990).

Lundstedt's point is clear: student-athletes are motivated to make a concerted effort in academic work. Such motivation acts as the bridge through which one area of keen interest helps to improve another area of lesser concern.

Sports & the Democratic/Individual Achievement Principle

The issue of individual achievement is central to the idea of equality. Individual achievement must be at potentially available to all its citizens before a community can have a spirit of equality. Without examples of individuals from different backgrounds having equal opportunities to pursue personal achievements, the idea of equal liberties grows dimmer. We need a paradigm of such hopeful possibilities, open to all racial, cultural, religious, and socio-economic backgrounds, that can be readily observed and understood by all citizens.

Sports provide, on a regular basis, the closest paradigm for all to see of the democratic achievement principle. Every week and, during the summer baseball season, every day, whether heard over the radio or seen on television or in person, there are continuous examples of individuals from all backgrounds exercising the individual achievement principle. In various sports, we observe people participating equally and modeling efforts to achieve self-improvement. In sports, we have a constant reminder of the vision inherent in the Constitution's ideal for each of us: a vision that holds true if we are but given the opportunity to pursue that ideal of individual achievement within the common good.

As I discussed in the last chapter, sports participation cuts across individual and group differences. More than any other single type of activity in our country, participation in sports demands the same involvement from all participants. Whether your skin is black, white, yellow, brown or red, no matter what your religion or where you live, sports participation demands that you run, jump, cry, sweat, bleed, and work alone and with teammates in the same manner as all other participants. Likewise, sports participation demands that a player wear the same type of equipment and perform under the same regulations and on the same court or field as any other participant, regardless of his or her racial, religious, political background, and past or current socio-economic status. No other single type of activity in our country exemplifies or promotes the principle of equality of opportunity and individual achievement principle as much as sports activities. Their language, required behaviors, and physical demands are universal in their application to participants.

R.D. Mandell (1986, 283) summarizes the great equalizing effect of sports in democratic societies:

> Modern sport encourages and demonstrates democratic achievement principle. Indeed it is not incontestable (as it never was before our time) that measurable, superior accomplishment (and nothing else) ought to be the basis of material reward. It is a principle of democratic societies that opportunities to strive for rewards should be equally accessible to each person at birth...

Obviously, we have a long way to go to resolve all issues of social inequalities and interracial disharmony in America. However, wouldn't it be great if the media would broadcast positive information on a frequent basis about cooperative interactions between African-Americans, Caucasian-Americans, Hispanic-Americans, Asian-Americans, Native-Americans, and any other ethnic group working together with members of other ethnic groups?

This is not to deny that we need to know about cases of injustice where they exist. However, we can learn of the potential for increased interracial harmony by being exposed to examples of the many that occur daily in our nation; examples that are eclipsed by all the negative information presented each day through the media. But when do you hear a sports announcer say "The White quarterback throws a pass to his Black receiver who is tackled by the Samoan linebacker"? Never. And that is because sports participation is color-blind...and a perfect example of presenting racial harmony as the norm, not the exception.

The old saying "Out of sight out of mind" applies to this scenario. In race relations, focusing on the negative and ignoring the positive long enough can promote the development of the "Pygmalion effect": people tend to act in a manner consistent with the expectations of others (Waterman, 1988, 12). That is, if people of one ethnic group are exposed long enough to more negative than positive information about another group, it's not unlikely that the first group will be less than enthusiastic about openly communicating with the second group. Such frequent negative impressions often obviate the best of hopeful efforts to integrate groups. Millions of interracial cooperative efforts take place in America every day. Unfortunately, news regarding interracial activities that receive top billing too often focuses on negative events instead of the many more positive situations.

The reality is that for the majority of Americans, sports activities provide the most frequent models of cooperation among people of different races and cultural backgrounds. To observe people of various skin colors and cultural backgrounds playing together in a symphony orchestra, or acting in a stage play together, allows us to see the larger possibilities for integration throughout society. But, because of their popularity, sports coverage in the media generally provides us with the most regular and positive examples of successful interracial cooperation in our country.

There is an urgent need to resolve socioeconomic discrepancies in our inner cities. It does not matter, though, how much money is poured into such relief efforts as building businesses, with an eye towards increasing jobs and renewing neighborhoods, if a spirit of cooperation is not first developed. Such a spirit must first be envisioned. To accomplish this, we need examples of interracial cooperation, and sports provide the most frequently observed examples. Fortunately, the same spirit of cooperation is similarly fostered by other co-curricular activities.

Values & Vision Promoted by Co-curricular Participation

America is the collective of its citizens in pursuit of an idea. It is a vision conceived by the founding fathers of the twofold principle, anchored by law: to cherish individual freedoms while protecting the good of the entire community.

When the founding fathers initiated this nation, they recognized the weaknesses inherent in any system of government organized by mortals. Wary of government that hinged on the varying and precarious determinations of men, their greatest concerns, as noted earlier, was that the new nation would be ruled by law, not men. With weaknesses still to be corrected, we can take heart that the words spoken by John F. Kennedy over 31 years ago still hold true today: "Freedom has many difficulties, and democracy is not perfect, but we have never had to put a wall up to keep our people in, to prevent them from leaving" (Bennett, 1989, 212).

Our ability to maintain freedoms in America, including the freedom to leave, is closely tied to the reason that relatively few of our citizens choose to leave and millions of foreigners wish to enter our borders: there exists in America a vision of freedom.

The agreement to disagree is central to any democracy. But a common vision of freedom and other basic principles outlined in our Constitution precede any such agreements. This common vision acts as a beacon for all to pursue, individually and collectively. There are differences regarding the ways in which people pursue this "beacon" of freedom - that is where civil rules, or laws, become operative. But our individual and collective efforts to pursue freedom, guided and restrained by popularly-determined law, take place according to our shared vision of freedom.

In *The Good Society*, authors Robert Bellah et al. (1991, 138-139) help us understand the significance of vision in maintaining bonds of unity while allowing for the pursuit of different interests, a balance so fundamental to our democracy:

> A mass of claimants organized into various pressure groups is not a public. There is nothing wrong with interests and nothing wrong with having them represented. But democratic government is more than the compromising of conflicting interests...Compromise...is not enough...The eighteenth century idea of a public was not just a congeries of interest groups but a discursive community capable of thinking about the common good...

Often our politicians and political parties debase the public by playing on its desires and fears: desire for private benefits at the expense of public provision; fear of just those most in need of public provision. What we need is precisely the opposite: a vision of how we are indeed dependent on and jointly responsible for a common life...

The simultaneous pursuit of individual and mutual improvement in school sports participation and other co-curricular activities is the embodiment of the duadic principle of our Constitution, and the vision to which Bellah et al. refer. The vision of a democratic society is one in which individuals have a chance to better themselves but not to the detriment of the group. It is a vision which encourages individuals to try to improve themselves while concurrently contributing to the community's growth. The symbiotic ideal of collateral growth of individuals (players) and the community (sports team or other co-curricular group) is constantly reenacted by student sports participants.

Two former U.S. Presidential Cabinet members help us focus the lense regarding the cultivation of a common vision and values. John W. Gardner was Secretary of Health, Education, and Welfare from 1965 to 1968, and later served as Director of the National Urban Coalition from 1968 to 1970. William J. Bennett served as U.S. Secretary of Education from 1985 to 1988, and as Director of the National Drug Control Policy from 1988 to 1991. Now a professor at the Stanford University Business School, Gardner (1990, 13) alerts us to the vulnerability of values: "Values always decay over time. Societies that keep their values alive do so not by accepting the process of decay but by powerful processes of regeneration."

Bennett (1988, 12) echoes Gardner's warning by quoting the philosopher and social critic, Sidney Hook: "Unless that faith and that belief [in liberal democracy] can be restored and revivified, liberal democracy will perish."

Bennett then follows up with a question and observation of his own to further clarify the point:

How, then, do we restore and revivify our faith in liberal democracy? A good place to start, the best place to start is with the education of our young. Many of the intellectual and moral failures we are now experiencing are the logical outcome of not teaching students the differences between democracy and other, less worthy forms of government, of not teaching students why they should cherish democratic ide-

als. Children are not born knowing these things instinctively; a love of
democratic principles, and an understanding of why they are so important, must be taught explicitly. They must be taught in the schools of
any democracy that wishes to survive. They must be passed from generation to generation (212). A man is not free to plan and design what
he has not learned or thought of (148).

The values which bind a people together must be kept alive with
timely examples on a regular basis. People living in a nation who are
expected to know the values on which the nation is based, and to live
accordingly, will not be able to do so unless they are given opportunities
to observe and experience those values. Again, this is an "Out of sight,
out of mind" dynamic.

Our schools, as the primary agents of socialization, are positioned
most naturally to involve youth in programs that will teach them the values of our Constitution. The classroom is the ideal place to teach and
discuss the theory of the Constitution. Co-curricular programs are the
ideal activities for students to voluntarily experience and practice cooperative interaction while pursuing their own individual achievement,
which, again, is the twofold principle of the Constitution.

Returning to the old saying in commercial marketing discussed in
chapter 1, we see its application to contemporary problems of youth and
other social concerns: "You have to get them into the store before they
will buy!" Every day throughout the school year, the majority of American youth convene at our schools, as mandated by law. In fact we do not
have to constantly go out and round up these prospective "buyers"; they
show up!

And what do we hope they "buy"?

First of all, we hope that they will "buy" the vision encompassing the
principles of our Constitution. That is not to say that we should aim for
our youth to "buy" everything that   America has been or is currently.
Rather, we hope they will "buy" the democratic principles which continually operate and evolve within the Constitution. We hope they will
"buy" the American spirit of cherishing individual freedoms and rights
within the overarching claims of the community, and the hope which
this twofold principle holds out to us.

Second, we hope they will "buy" information that will help them improve themselves and that will allow them to learn cooperation with others of all racial, cultural, religious, political, and socio-economic backgrounds.

Once they show up, however, it is a matter of getting them to participate in the learning process. It is up to the educators, public servants,
American adult public, and particularly parents, to provide our youth
with the conditions and incentives to stimulate their desire to learn. In
general, it is up to adult citizens, with the leadership of our policymakers,
to provide our youth with the environment and programs that help them
acquire the mental, physical, and social skills that will contribute to their
growth, individually and collectively, and to the regeneration of our national community.

In school sports, we have such valuable programs. In addition to being agents of promoting the vision of our democratic ideals, school sports
have a natural appeal to millions of youth of all backgrounds. This appeal
can be a powerful conduit to increasing interest in academic subjects and
classroom efforts, as suggested earlier by Stanford's Dr. Nel Noddings,
Independence High School principal, Dr. John Sallarole, and teacher,
Beverly Lundstedt.

In chapter 5, I described how such programs have been successfully
implemented in the Biddy Basketball League conducted by the Children's
Aid Society in New York City. Ironically, as widespread need for such
programs has substantially grown over the past quarter century, funding
has been progressively diminished. School sports and other co-curricular
programs can be great assets to the American public (shopkeepers) to
prompt students to "buy" (accept and learn) the merchandise offerings
(our democratic vision and education in general). In so doing, these programs contribute to the renewing of the significant values established by
the founding fathers, which are continually adapted to meet emerging
needs of subsequent generations.

Regeneration from Generation to Generation

Any organism, individual or collective, must be able to regenerate its
essential, life-sustaining elements to continue living. Similarly, a nation
will be able to continue to the extent that it can renew its essential life-
sustaining qualities (values on which it is based) through activities which
nurture and strengthen those qualities. School sports and other co-curricular programs provide youth with such activities, on a voluntary basis,
that are connected to their required educational experience. John Gardner's
(1964) comparison of organic and social renewal in his book, *Self-Re-*

newal, helps to illuminate the capacities of school sports to promote and regenerate our Constitutional values.

Prefacing his observations, Dr. Gardner (1964) notes that occasionally a new discovery of a lost civilization is made, which tends to prompt wonderings among the living if their own culture will also eventually meet extinction. Since all social organizations mature and decay with the passing of time, Gardner poses the engaging question: "Suppose one tried to imagine a society that would be relatively immune to decay - an ever-renewing society. What would it be like (1-7)?" He responds to his own question, by suggesting that a surviving society would need to have the capacity for continuous innovation, renewal and re-birth. In other words, it must be a system which constantly facilitates a process of continuity as well as change.

But it is difficult for most of us to imagine such a picture, because our thinking of growth and decline in living organisms is "...dominated by the image of a single life-span, animal or vegetable. Seedling, full flower and death." To suggest what a surviving, continuously renewing social community would look like, Gardner replaces the single life-span metaphor with an alternative one:

...for an ever-renewing society the appropriate image is total garden, a balanced aquarium or other ecological system. Some things are being born, other things are flourishing, still other things are dying - but the system lives on (1-7).

Gardner's metaphorical garden as a maturing yet enduring and re-generating system is a dynamic allegory of what our Constitution was intended to be. As the founding fathers allowed for in its design, the Constitution has been amended 26 times to allow for the unknown changes they anticipated as being an inevitable part of the ever-fluctuating life process. They did not know what specific changes would develop, but they wisely anticipated the eventuality of change...much as the athlete, or any other co-curricular participant, must anticipate inevitable yet unpredictable stochastic changes continually experienced and modelled in sports and other co-curricular activities.

For any social system to be self-renewing, its citizens must willingly support its values and participate in its continuance. There needs to be activities in which values are regularly and frequently played out and are commonly experienced by its citizens...voluntarily!

Sports participation, both direct (players) and indirect (observers, fans), is such an activity. More than any other type of activity, sports participation brings people together from completely different backgrounds to commonly experience the duadic principle of our Constitution: individual rights and achievement (individual players), pursued within the good of the community (team) by conforming to a system of justice (agreed-upon rules enforced by the game officials).

Again, the process of regeneration requires activities which facilitates a process of continuity as well as change. In school sports, we have voluntary activities that can be implemented to stimulate individual academic efforts, individual and group adaptation to change, and to promote continuity and community by bridging the differences between participants.

Because they are so valuable to our youth and our country, we will now review in detail the community-building and renewing features of school sports and other co-curricular programs.

School Sports and Community Renewal

In *On Leadership*, Dr. Gardner (1990) lists eight attributes, characteristic of successful communities, which actually facilitate the continuous innovation and regeneration that is required for a social organization to continuously survive. Although he stipulates that this list is arguable, all are well thought-out principles that provide a framework to further consider the important contributions of school sports to the process of community renewal. Six of those attributes are present in and encouraged by school sports and other co-curricular activities. Following is a description of each attribute, and an analysis of its applicability to school sports participation.

1. Wholeness Incorporating Diversity

> A community is obviously less of a community if fragmentation or divisiveness exists - and if the rifts are deep, it is no community at all...We expect and want diversity, and there is dissension in the best of communities. But vital communities face and resolve differences...(116).

As discussed earlier, individuals need to coalesce around rallying points of common concern or values for there to be community. This is particularly true today as we have moved from an industrial society to an information society according to Alvin Toffler (1991) and John Naisbitt and Patricia Aburdeen (1985). These authors explain that the primary resources on which we depended as an industrial society were cash or cash equivalents. Today, however, human capacities, in the forms of knowledge and creativity have replaced cash equivalents as the main resources for our socio-economic welfare.

As a result, development and coordination of human resources has become the chief focus of achieving future success in business and all other organizations. Cooperation and teamwork are essential for organizational and individual success in the new information society.

This new emphasis on development of human resources and coalescing of individuals into cooperative teams coincides with Robert Waterman's observations in *The Renewal Factor: How the Best Get and Keep the Competitive Edge*, which included the importance of teamwork and cooperation in order to maximize human resource development. More and more, corporations are moving away from the vertical hierarchical organizational structure so much identified with traditional industrial society. Instead, they are structuring their organizations in a more horizontal type of structure, one in which there is less hierarchical interaction and more lateral, interdependent and cooperative actions and interactions taking place, as everyone is asked to contribute information. Hence, business organizations have an increasing need for employees who have interactive skills as well as technical abilities.

The emphasis of school sports on cooperation, sacrifice for the good of the team, and equality provided by a "level playing field" promotes social integration and encourages interactive skills needed by business organizations. Participation in school sports involves continued efforts to improve individually and as a team, regardless of diversity in the backgrounds of team members. Consequently, participation in school sports reflects the spirit expressed in the first paragraph of Archibald MacLeish's essay, "America Is Always Still to Build":

> America is a country of extremes. Those who think she should be all of a piece, all of a kind...every house like its neighbor and all minds alike, have never traveled on this continent. American wholeness, American singleness, American strength, is the wholeness, the singleness, the strength of many opposites made one. The Republic is a symbol of union because it is also a symbol of differences, and it will endure, not

because its deserts and sea coasts and forests and bayous and dead
volcanoes are of one mind, but because they are several minds and are
nevertheless together...

2. A Shared Culture

The possibility of wholeness is considerably enhanced if the community has a shared culture, that is, shared norms and values... symbols
of group identity and its story which it retells often. Social cohesion is
advanced if the group's norms and values are explicit. Values that are
never expressed are apt to be taken for granted and not adequately con-
veyed to young people and newcomers. The well-functioning community provides many opportunities to express values in relevant action
(116).

Again, as I noted at the outset of this chapter in the quotations by
Winston Churchill and John W. Gardner, all civilizations begin with a
vision. Members of a community must generally agree to a vision of
some basic values or ideals by which the community will determine standards of acceptable behaviors. Without a common vision of what behaviors are and are not acceptable, individuals within a community run in
their own directions, with little regard for those of others. A common
vision provides the connecting link, however loose that connection may
at times be, among the different people within the community. Such vision acts as a basic reference point or steering mechanism for a community. It is the social rudder which enables a sailing ship of community to
stay the course through the turbulence of stochastic currents and storms.

Shared vision of common norms and values played an important role
in the institution of our nation. Forming a new Constitution in the late
eighteenth century was a monumental task. When the founding fathers
completed the framework of our Constitution, a few factors had made the
task an even greater challenge. For one thing, most American families
were generally quite isolated from each other on a daily basis. As 96% of
the population in 1787 lived on farms, communication between Americans was particularly difficult. In addition, differences existed among the
citizens of the recently liberated colonies-turned independent states, from
pro-slavery and anti-slavery disputes to political issues such as taxation,
representation, and territorial claims.

Despite these points of discord, there was much more to unify Americans than to divide them. The most prevalent unifying factor, of course,

was their common foe, England. The Revolution had bridged any major differences among the separate colonies. Freedom from the tyrannical rule of Mother England had forged a filial bond between most Americans which counteracted and precluded potential conflicts.

Here we can see the unifying power of common vision. As the colonists commonly held the vision of victory over the oppressive rule of England, they worked, fought, were wounded and died in battle together, all towards achieving that vision. Where they did have differences, they put them aside to achieve their mutually shared vision of self-rule. Their goal of national independence was precipitated by their vision of it. This type of common purpose and commitment is not unlike that voluntarily practiced in school sports and other co-curricular activities. To achieve individual team goals, individual differences are voluntarily put aside, at least temporarily. And where individual concerns are precluded even temporarily by those of the group, the individual has an opportunity to experience teammates on a common footing - like the early colonists from slave states were able to do when fighting with those from anti-slave states in the cause against the British.

Similarly, the Constitution was a result of a common vision, one of shared hope by its framers. *Time* Magazine's Roger Rosenblatt (1987, 21) captures the essence of that shared vision in his following commentary on the Constitution as literature:

> The Constitution is more than literature, but as literature, it is primarily a work of the imagination. It imagined a country: fantastic. More fantastic still, it imagined a country full of people imagining themselves. Within the exacting articles and stipulations there was not only room to fly but also the tacit encouragement to fly, even the instructions to fly, traced delicately within the solid triangular concoction (the three separate branches of government coordinated and regulated by the system of checks and balances) of the framers. Even 200 years after the fact, when people debate whether the Constitution is fit for so complicated and demanding a time, Americans take as granted the right to grow into themselves. They must have read it somewhere, in a fable.

Visionaries are those individuals who can see long-term possibilities through a landscape littered with limited perspectives and current circumstances. As Rosenblatt observes, the amazing thing about the vision incorporated in the Constitution by its visionary framers is that it was one which "imagined" its citizens "imagining themselves." For over 200 years, the focus of that self-imagining has been hope: hope for a good and, perhaps, a better, tomorrow. Through its continued revision, via 26 amendments, it has continued to be a document of hope, which is why there are constantly millions trying to come into our country but few are trying to leave.

A link can be seen between the vision pursued in the Constitution and that which is regularly experienced in school sports: a group of people voluntarily striving for their individual advancement as well as the common good. It is endeavoring for self-improvement and contributing to that of the community at the same time which is complementary to and reflective of, the ideals expressed in the U.S. Constitution.

While a human culture is a large grouping of people who share similar customs and ways of doing things, those shared ways are subject to the same law of life observed by John F. Kennedy, noted at the beginning of chapter 4: the law of change. Over time, cultures must adapt to unpredictable changes, referred to as "stochastic shocks" in chapter 4. As also pointed out in that chapter, school sports participation necessitates adaptation to the changes which constantly occur during such participation. At an early age, youth are provided valuable voluntary experiences to deal with such stochastic changes.

But how does this voluntary learning experience, on an individual and small group basis among youth, in adaptation to change relate to cultural adaptations to life changes?

Similar to the metaphorical model of hope presented by sports in our culture, school sports provide an arena, regardless of individual ethnic, religious, racial or economic backgrounds in which to practice the twofold principle that underpins our Constitution: pursuing the individual achievement within the common good as anchored by law. School sports provide a common vision of mutual striving for individual and group improvement. The key value of sports participation, as far as adaptation to change is concerned, is that participants continue to practice this duadic principle together, as a team, regardless of individual differences and in the face of unexpected changes. In the face of stochastic changes, participants are required to obey the law (game rules) in their attempt to improve themselves and their teammates without regard to individual background differences. The same thing is generally required of participants in other co-curricular programs.

The following observations of John Gardner (1991, 13) underscore the critical need for activities such as school sports and other co-curricu-

lar programs to regularly present a vision of shared values for community renewal:

> A great civilization is a drama lived in the minds of a people. It is
> a shared vision; it is shared norms, expectations, and purposes...A com-
> munity lives in the minds of its members - in shared assumptions, be-
> liefs, customs, ideas that give meaning, ideas that motivate...In any
> healthy, reasonably coherent community, people come to have shared
> views concerning right and wrong, better and worse - in personal con-
> duct, in governing, in art, whatever...

Although struggles continue with issues of social injustice such as
racism, hope has continued to exist as changes have been made, albeit
not numerous nor fast enough. Among segments of our population who
have been limited in the freedoms and opportunities originally provided
in the Constitution are Blacks and women. Yes, the Thirteenth Amendment abolishing slavery should have been included from the start. And,
yes, the Nineteenth Amendment giving women the right to vote was much
too late. But, because of the founders' provision for amending the Constitution, these changes were made. We have a long way to go in resolving civil and social inequities in the United States. However, hope is kept
alive within the ideals expressed in the Constitution and by changes that
have been made in that document over time. It is a vision that we share,
and experiences that bring us together in common, such as those provided by school sports and other co-curricular programs, that fan the flames
of hope despite many individual differences among our people.

The visions of hope fostered by the Constitution and promoted and
experienced via school sports participation are captured in the following
statement by Charlayne Hunter-Gault. As the first African-American who
was admitted to the University of Georgia in 1961, by court order, her
testimony regarding the Constitution's provision of hope is important,
meaningful and, in itself, hopeful:

> In some of the darkest hours when racism and sexism seem to be
> winning, one can maintain a sense of optimism because you know that
> there is recourse. No matter how dark it gets, it is not going to get pitch
> dark because there is that document [Constitution]. One doesn't see
> any light at the end of the tunnel in South Africa because its law says
> that Black people are inferior. Here we have perpetual light because of
> our Constitution (Time, 1987).

Hunter-Gault's words of perpetual light ring true when we see people of different racial backgrounds participate equally and cooperatively on one team against another in fairly conducted contests of school sports competition. Of course, the classic example of the equal opportunity presented by sports in general is Jackie Robinson's breakthrough entry into major league baseball in 1947. Although the ruling allows Black Americans to play in the major leagues was too long in coming, it was an eventuality; one that has taken even longer to transpire in other areas of our society in schools and other institutions.

Another hopeful perspective relative to adapting to life changes that is both characteristic of the provisions of our Constitution and promoted in school sports participation is voiced by syndicated newspaper columnist, Ellen Goodman (1987):

> I suppose that many American women have had a lopsided love affair with the Constitution. We've honored the concept of rule by law even when the law itself rejected us. It took 133 years just to win the vote denied by the Founding Fathers. We're still waiting for equal status. The beauty of the Constitution is that it gives permission, and approval, for change.

Again, it was the founding fathers's vision for the need to adapt to changing times, as "WE THE PEOPLE of the United States see fit," that is the rationale for the amendment process. And this vision has been adopted by the people to generally pursue commonly shared values, based on individual rights, within the common good. It is this vision of shared norms and values that is promoted by participation in school sports and other co-curricular programs.

3. Caring, Trust and Teamwork

> A good community nurtures its members and fosters an atmosphere of trust...Undergirding the teamwork is an awareness by all that they need one another and must pool their talent, and energy and resources. There is a feeling that when the team wins everybody wins (117).

When the terms "team" and "teamwork" are mentioned, we are usually reminded of an athletic team, players working together to achieve individual and group improvement and ultimately a game victory. The prospects of success in sports or any other worthwhile enterprise requires concerted effort of all those involved in its execution, with the graduation of student participants to subsequent grades, the level of sports competition increases, and the roles of second and third string players become ever more important to the success of the team. Most successful teams have second and third string players who strongly challenge first string players in practice. In doing so, they prepare themselves as well during practices in case they are called into a game to replace a starter; equally important, they help the starting cast of players prepare better for the team's next game opponent.

During the course of a season, team members are individually and collectively called upon to face the challenges of difficult physical and mental demands. They are required to sacrifice other activities in order to participate on the team. They sustain personal discomfort and pain to go the "extra mile" for the sake of the team. By doing all he or she can to not let the team down, an athlete or other co-curricular participant avoids letting himself or herself down. He or she pulls from within him- or herself the determination and strength to bear up against hardships for the sake of his or her teammates and, in the process, benefits more himself or herself as the individual comes to realize more of his or her own potential than he or she otherwise would have known existed.

4. Participation and the Sharing of Leadership Tasks

> The healthy community encourages individual involvement in the pursuit of shared purposes...whether in a city or an organization, the possibility of effective participation in considerably increased if everyone is kept informed, and if individuals feel that they have a say...The good community finds a productive balance between individuality and group obligation...Everyone need not participate with respect to any given community. We must guard the right to participate while recognizing that some will choose not to do so...(117).

Here again, the important aspect of voluntary participation is emphasized by Gardner. Voluntary participation is fundamental to co-curricular activities and to a democratic society.

While participation is voluntary in co-curricular programs, direction must be established and presided over by a common leader. In sports, the main leader is usually the coach. In the theater, it is the director, or the school's drama teacher. As emphasized in prior chapters, particularly in chapter 1, co-curricular mentors and coaches have significant opportunities to model positive values and provide direction to students.

The term "leader" is usually thought of in connection with one individual who organizes, directs, motivates or otherwise influences group members to act in a particular manner. In these capacities, coaches and mentors of co-curricular activities exercise a great deal of responsibility in directing the voluntary student participants in their respective programs. These mentors can significantly influence the development of their students positively or negatively, depending on the mentors' attitude and actions. This influence, as emphasized earlier, is why coaches and mentors should be professionally trained in principles of education and human behavior as much as any classroom teacher or other professional working in education or human development.

But, while one or a limited number of mentors are commissioned with the primary task of orchestrating a school co-curricular group's activities, there are other members whose actions often end up aiding or assisting those of designated leaders. Such ancillary gestures of leadership usually involve satisfying the intangible needs of the team. These types of supportive actions include but are not limited to the following: "picking up the team spirit" and supporting the actions of team by demonstrating enthusiasm when others are "down" and when things do not go well; leading by example; exemplifying cooperation; committing to the team when tempted to quit in the face of adversity; and being willing to sacrifice individual needs and goals. It is through such positive examples in attitude and behavior as these that everyone can contribute to the leadership of a school team in sports, drama, band, newspaper, or any other group or social community. School sports and other co-curricular programs provide every participant with the opportunity to be proactive and to develop such leadership abilities.

5. Develop Young People

The opportunities for individual growth are numerous and varied for all members. And the mature members ensure that the young grow up with a sense of obligation to the community. Beginning in elementary and high school, boys and girls should learn to take some responsibility for the well-being of any group they are in - a seemingly small step but without a doubt the first step toward responsible community participation. On the playing field and in group activities in and out of school, teamwork can be learned...(118).

Whatever has been discussed so far regarding this attribute of "good community" is summarily reflected in the above words of John Gardner. School sports and other co-curricular activities provide students with ultimate opportunities to develop skills and attitudes vital to the building and regenerating community.

6. Links with the Outside World

> There is always a certain tension between the need for the community to draw boundaries to protect its integrity on the one hand, and the need to have fruitful links with the larger communities of which it is a part...(118).

Accordingly, co-curricular activities serve a natural function regarding this attribute of a "good community." The primary means for a school to be involved with other schools is when their sports teams play each other in a game. In fact, one of the primary ways in America for different communities to interact is when their respective sports teams play a game against each other. Of course, this takes place thousands of times each school year. In this way, school sports act as a model of interaction of communities - similar to interactions of different communities prompted by the original Olympic games of 2,500 years ago. In those ancient days, separate states of Greece temporarily called a truce in their wars for the sake of the Olympic games. This in itself is testimony to the age-old capacity of sports to bridge community differences.

As student co-curricular participants voluntarily practice the principles of democracy (the principle of individual achievement within the common good of the team, according to the rules equally required of all participants, regardless of individual differences), they simultaneously experience and model for others what a democratic community is all about: sharing, self-sacrifice, achieving, helping, receiving, giving, supporting, and being supported.

The experience and the model may often, if not always, be imperfect. No human institution is perfect. Yet, since the time of ancient Greece, sports participation embodies the practices that most closely resembles a life metaphor for building community. As I have repeatedly pointed out, no other single type of activity brings together as many people from diverse backgrounds to voluntarily and commonly participate in the completion of a task, the achievement of a common objective voluntarily as school sports. Then, this commonly experienced participation of people with differences within the school is extended to other communities during games between schools.

Of all the 6 attributes described by Gardner as characteristic of a "good community" which apply to co-curricular activities in schools, this is the one in which sports promotes more than other school programs. As I have emphasized, other co-curricular activities foster similar practices as school sports within school communities; but, by virtue of games being played between teams from schools located in different communities, interscholastic sports competition promote links with the outside world more frequently than other co-curricular programs.

Links with the outside world: co-curricular programs, particularly school sports, strongly advances this characteristic of a "good community" as suggested by Dr. John Gardner.

Chapter 7

Which Price Will We Pay?

Cutting athletics: save now, pay later!
- Thomas Boswell, *The Washington Post*

At the beginning of chapter 1, I referred to the old Fram oil filter television commercial to illustrate the price society pays regarding its programs for youth. When it comes to the oil system of a car, avoiding the smaller price of $15 for a new oil filter today is an unwise savings when one considers the far greater expenditure to be paid at a later date for repairs of resulting engine damage. Preventive maintenance has a much smaller price tag than remedial repairs or a completely overhauled engine.

Likewise, money saved at the expense of education today will eventually be spent in far greater multiples for jails, law enforcement and justice system costs tomorrow. Also, the same rationale for preventing breakdowns in the condition of an automobile applies to the physical, emotional and social health of human beings as we have reviewed in the first chapter. While the filter analogy poses a simple choice relative to a single automobile, we have a similar, albeit more complex, choice regarding our most important national resource, our youth. To be sure, we will continue to pay an ever-increasing price for social problems involving our youth as pointed out in chapter 1 by New York State Senator Alton R. Waldon, Jr. His observation is strongly borne out when we compare the annual expense of over $20,750 to maintain one prisoner in the California penal system to the approximately $5,000 per student expense in that state's public education system.

Regeneration Versus Diseased and Obsolescence

As we discussed in chapter 6, for any community to continue, it must develop the means not just to maintain itself but to regenerate itself. Drawing again upon Dr. John Gardner's metaphor of the garden of renewal , we see that our democratic society can continue only if we have programs in which the "seeds" of democracy are developed and cultivated in young people; programs in which youth have opportunities to practice democratic principles. Currently, the growth of our democratic, societal "garden" is being stunted by the "disease" of the social problems we discussed at length earlier, among which are: the continued breakdown of the family unit, implicit and explicit media promulgation of violence, mixed messages, and self-indulgent attitudes, which include irresponsible and frivolous sexual activity. Meanwhile, we have considerably cut back on available voluntary and constructive "seed" and preventive maintenance programs.

Truly, we are saving pennies now (by not funding these programs) only to have to pay a much higher price of replanting the entire "garden," if that will even be possible, or face its eventual demise. In either case, the ultimate cost far outweighs the current one...just like the car owner who saved $15 by not buying the oil filter but later spent many hundreds of dollars to overhaul his engine.

In our society, the two factors which have the greatest correlation with youth-related problems are the breakdown of the family and socio-economic disparities. But, in view of the complexities involved in resolving the negative influences of these social dilemmas, our schools have a difficult task at best in providing support systems to make up for the lack of adult and family support so greatly needed by millions of our youth. There are no panaceas for our social ills that will completely and immediately regenerate our societal "garden." No educational nor any other formula can provide a total cure-all for our problems related to education and our youth.

However, the benefits provided by school sports and other co-curricular programs are and can be stronger components of remedial and preventive efforts in helping millions of youth become positively directed. The effective combination of these voluntary learning activities with the study of core curriculum subjects can be implemented, in terms of John Gardner's social garden metaphor, as components of a larger "social horticultural" program: a program that would help regenerate our American societal garden. Both educational components would contribute to the larger program of social renewal by "cultivating, planting, and nurturing" among our youth the "seeds" of individual and collaborative attitudes and behaviors necessary for the renewing and improving of our society.

In addition to providing greater support to education in general and, in particular, for poor children, Marian Wright Edelman (1991), president of the Children's Defense Fund, contends that we need to provide high-quality after school programs to supplement what is taught in schools. Within the context of our oil filter metaphor, her plea for increased support for the expansion of these youth programs according to her makes a great deal of sense:

> ...If political leaders don't blink about bailing out savings and loan institutions to the tune of at least $160 billion or spending $1 billion a day on the Persion Gulf War, why should we blink about insisting that they bail children and families out of poverty at a cost of $20 billion annually (Wright Edelman, 1991).

Neither Marian Wright Edelman nor I have illusions that, by itself, funding these programs will be the complete answer. However, we both agree that significant improvements will be made toward resolving youth problems if programs are implemented to achieve her suggestions. Furthermore, widely-supported voluntary school programs, directed by well-qualified mentors, will greatly help in directing youth away from subtle and blatant destructive activities that have been so much on the rise.

A large part of the example that we should be setting for youth is in the very act of properly providing for their welfare and preparing them to be responsible citizens. Co-curricular programs will go a long way in supplementing the core curricula towards that end. Such programs are mutually reinforcing and complementary, as claimed by the various educators identified in this work. As previously stated, I make no claim that voluntary co-curricular activities should be supported in lieu of mandated core curricular courses. On the contrary, both curricula are important to the development of our youth resources, and they are mutually complementary and reinforcing!

Programs combining core and co-curricular activities are effectively being used, on a small scale, in remedial projects aimed at decreasing gang involvements and other youth-related problems. The Biddy Basketball League in New York City is one example, as described in chapter 5.

Another such recent program is called the "Empowerment of Hispanic Students and Their Families," which was initiated in the East Side Union High School District of San Jose, CA for the 1991-'92 school year. In addition to tutoring and counseling services, the program includes

"...after school sports programs offering students a safe place to go at night and on weekends" (Ramos, 1991). Currently these programs involve little or no coaching, due to limited funds. But the program director, Dr. John Fernandez (1992), notes that these activities would have far more positive effects on your participants with proper coaching available.

As youth problems continue to increase in America, it is indeed ironic that support for school sports, which were recognized during the first half of the twentieth century for their ability to dissuade youth from socially deviant activities, has been decreased as youth problems continue to increase. The same types of programs praised by President Teddy Roosevelt back in 1893, and implemented upon the recommendation by the National Education Association's famous "Cardinal Principles of Secondary Education" report in 1918, have been proven effective even in contemporary times, according to all the professionals in education, social work, and law enforcement with whom I consulted. Yet they are now being cast as nonessential.

Because educational programs involving both core curricula and co-curricula are important to the development of our youth, the question naturally arises, Where will the activities for co-curricular participation be made available if they are not provided by our schools in tandem with core curricula? The answer is that these activities cannot be conducted anywhere else as effectively as in our schools. Most schools have already been built with the facilities to accommodate the integration of these programs. In addition, teacher training programs in our colleges have been developed to educate mentors in principles of human behavior as it relates to education of youth.

American public schools were commissioned from the beginning of this century to implement such programs to address the similar types of youth problems as those we face today. We have a tremendous opportunity to reinstate high-quality sports and other co-curricular programs with full-time teachers who are also properly trained as coaches and mentors.

Technology and "Me" Versus Community and the Whole Person

Since the post-World War II nuclear scare of the 1950's, accompanied by the 45 year "cold war" and the successful Soviet launch of Sputnik I, the United States emphasized technological and scientific knowledge over that of social sciences. Also, as I described earlier, as educational budgets have been cut over the past thirty years, areas considered to be less essential to the moon race and winning the cold war were tabbed for the cutting board. These areas usually came from the social/experiential/athletic domain.

The good news is that we won both the cold war and the moon race. The bad news is that, for the noble cause of winning these technological wars, we have made crucial errors along the way, sacrificing important educational programs which promote the development of cooperation among youth. As increased emphasis was placed on qualitative, scientific, and other core curricular subjects, co-curricular programs began to be deemphasized, as indicated by progressive funding cuts in these areas. One of the most unfortunate consequences of this event can be seen in motivation and stability in the lives of many youth.

At a time in which the family and the church, traditionally two of America's strongest institutions for the moral and motivational development of youth, have steadily been weakened in their ability to positively influence our youth, we need constructive co-curricular programs more than ever. Educational programs in which youth voluntarily participate, develop a sense of direction, and establish camaraderie with mentors and peers who care are significant needs of young people. And, as Tracy Robinson, Coordinator of the Gang Enforcement Unit of the Los Angeles City Attorney's Office, describes in chapter 1 of this book, youth will seek to fulfill such needs in youth gangs if they are not otherwise met.

Education funding cuts eliminating co-curricular programs have left a wide gap in many important experiences for youth. In the wake of the erosion of the family, the schools have inherited the primary duties of socialization, duties which had been the domain of the nuclear family in recent history and, before that, of the extended family for much of man's history.

Unfortunately, as I described at length in chapter 1, public schools (many private schools, for that matter) have adopted an open-ended approach to teaching moral principles of behavior, usually referred to as values clarification. In fact, this approach involved discussion instead of instruction, and emphasized student choice of right behavior versus wrong behavior. Instead of being instructed in traditional values by presenting examples of noteworthy individuals living those principles, students over the past 25 years have been encouraged to determine their own principles of right and wrong. As a result, schools have been limited in their efforts to fill the gap in this important aspect of socialization of our youth.

Two other influences have exacerbated the situation, as discussed in detail in chapter 1: (a) mixed messages within families and the media, and (b) media programs which encourage behavior devoid of behavior principles. Indeed, programs which involve students in activities that promote clear standards for appropriate behavior are greatly needed. Voluntary co-curricular programs help, at least partially, to fill the void.

For the welfare and development of our youth, the need for voluntary educational activities which reinforce and can promote required school programs in our schools has never been greater. Co-curricula help keep students from dropping out of school and provide students and faculty visible opportunities for common participation. These activities also prompt improved classroom behavior and academic efforts, as illustrated in chapter 1.

Never before have we needed co-curricular activities, which promote and reinforce the principles of our Constitution, renew community, and break down racial and socio-economic barriers, as much as we do at the present time. Our schools are strengthened by co-curricular programs; such programs reinforce schools in their ability to constructively empower youth and provide opportunities for the affiliation and direction so greatly needed by young people. Co-curricular activities provide youth with alternative visions of hope and positive involvements to choose over the negative, destructive ones, in gangs, to which so many have had to resort to satisfy these needs.

As important as co-curricular programs are to youth during their years in school, such programs also prove to be beneficial to youth in their post-school years. As discussed at length in chapter 3, opportunities provided by these programs allow students while they are in school to voluntarily learn and practice attitudes and behaviors which are vital to business and other organizations as well as our economic system of free enterprise.

Now that we have won the nuclear arms and space races, we should draw upon at least some of the peace dividend money from these technological victories to reinstate and better fund more educational programs, both required and voluntary. In turn, we will avoid much greater future costs in law enforcement, justice, and penal system expenditures, as well as decreased productivity: all would-be by-products of increased youth problems and eventual adult crimes, as juvenile delinquents become seasoned offenders. Again, I refer to Maria Wright Edelman's observation quoted above regarding our governmental "leaders bailing out savings and loan institutions with more than $160 billion." If funding can be mustered for that type of business mismanagement, and yet we are unable to fund valuable learning programs for our nation's youth, we will later pay a much higher price than any incurred by the savings and loan debacle.

Co-curricular Programs and Our Free Enterprise System

Because our democratic political system is fueled by the free enterprise system, private business is the central agent of that system. Without successfully operated businesses in the private sector, our democracy could not survive. As government intervention increases in the economic processes of a country, socialistic policies also increase. Our schools should strongly emphasize programs which introduce and encourage the practice of personal and interpersonal attitudes, behaviors, and skills required by free enterprise and private industry. And it is important to make such programs available on a voluntary basis, since our democracy is based on free choice; i.e., in America, a citizen can choose to freely participate in our nation as a citizen or as an employee as long as he or she agrees to live by the rules. We are free to choose the employment for which we are qualified and wish to pursue. And we can move to another country if we wish to do that; we are not forced to live in the United States. No matter what we freely choose, however, there are rules by which we must participate - just as in co-curricular participation.

Both individual initiative and teamwork are required to achieve social harmony in a community as well as for business organizations to realize economic profitability. As the need for greater verbal as well as technical skills increases in the future, so will the need for improved interpersonal and collaborative skills. They are regularly and voluntarily practiced on a mutual and equal basis in co-curricular programs.

The greatest concern expressed by business leaders today regarding employees who are newly hired out of schools is a lack of interpersonal and teamwork skills. This trend among new employees has resulted in lost profits due to downtime in operations, more time involved in training, and lower-level quality in performance. As more and more business functions require networking and communications among employees at various levels of a business's hierarchical structure, communications skills that used to be functional for the lowest level of operations are becoming increasingly outmoded. Consolidation of business functions resulting from computerization of these operations prompt greater need for effective communication and networking (i.e., teamwork) than ever before.

Among the strongest of recommendations made by the MIT Commission on Industrial Productivity, as reported in *Made in America: Regaining the Productive Edge* by Dertouzos et al. (1989) was the need to emphasize both individualism and cooperation. The report stressed that schools should have programs which provide opportunities for and encourage both individual achievement and collaborative efforts. In addition, the report called for both individual and cooperative efforts to be mutually recognized and appreciated. As we discussed in chapter 4, school sports provide a proactive means toward individual empowerment, and prompt interaction and collaboration with other individuals: the twofold goal suggested by the MIT Commission on Industrial Productivity.

Which Price Will We Pay?

In chapter 5, we discussed the observations of *The Washington Post* reporter, Tom Boswell (1992), of the strong correlation between the decline of support in school sports and increased youth problems. In the same article, Boswell presents a poignant perspective regarding our social problems, and then he asks a formidable question we can choose to ignore - but not without an eventual, much greater price to pay:

> Many of our social problems are as big and complex as they are obvious. We all know that more jobs, stronger families and better education would be forces for order. Yet knowing these problems still leaves us far from solutions. Increasing support for school sports... may be one small part of the large mosaic of restoring order to the lives of our young people. But, it is one part, isn't it? And, of all parts, isn't it by far the least costly, the least controversial, and the easiest to implement?

Boswell's last question is easy to answer. As I emphasized, our schools have already been built with the needed facilities. Our teacher-education programs have been established for many years to properly screen and train educators in coaching and mentoring. These training programs are available to help teachers-to-be develop skills in the appropriate disciplines to coach or mentor children as full-time professionals. Our youth deserve professionally trained teachers. And, because youth are truly our most valuable assets for the renewal and continuance of our nation, they should be instructed by full-time professionals in all areas of their educational experience. We have more than ample knowledge that the money we save in education today will be repaid many times over.

As only one but a considerably large part of the mosaic of solutions to our growing social problems, cultivating high quality school sports and other co-curricular programs is a relatively small price to pay to avoid the higher price we are currently paying due to youth-related problems. It is a particularly small price to pay when compared to the $160 billion of public money spent by Congress on the savings and loan travesty. And, as I detailed in chapter 1, it is an even smaller price to pay to avoid the geometrically larger price we will pay later in law enforcement, jails and the justice system, remedial programs for youthful offenders of the law, as well as the costs related to lost productivity; isn't it?

The choice is ours: we can pay a smaller price now for the many valuable benefits to youth and our nation provided by school sports and co-curricular programs. Or, we can pay a much greater price later. Which price will we choose to pay?

References

Baker, William J., *Sports in the Western World*, University of Illinois Press, Champaign, IL, 1988.

Bandura, Albert, *Social Learning Theory*, Prentice-Hall, Englewood Cliffs, NJ, 1977.

Barber, Benjamin, and Watson, Patrick, *The Struggle for Democracy*, Little, Brown & Co., Boston, 1988.

Bellah, Robert N.; Madsen, Richard; Sullivan, William M.; Swindler, Ann; and, Tipton, Steven M.; *The Good Society*, Alfred A. Knopf Publishers, New York, 1991.

Bennett, William J., *Our Children and Our Country*, Touchstone Books div. of Simon and Schuster Publishers, New York, 1989.

Boswell, Thomas, "Cutting Athletics: Save Now, Pay Later," *The Washington Post*, June 17, 1992, p. D-1.

Boyler, Rev. Gregory J. , S. J. , "Self-Esteem: A Matter of Life, Death," *Los Angeles Times*, January 28, 1990, p. M7.

California State Department of Corrections, *California Prisoners & Parolees 1991*, Offender Information Services Branch, Sacramento, CA 1991.

Cetron, Marvin, and Davies, Owen, *American Renaissance,* St. Martin's Press, New York, 1989.

Cetron, Marvin, and Gayle, Margaret, *Educational Renaissance*, St. Martin's Press, New York, 1991.

Coats, Hon. Dan, "America's Youth: A Crisis of Character," *American Family Association Journal*, November/December 1991, pp. 18-21.

Cousins, Norman, *Anatomy of an Illness*, W. W. Norton, New York, 1979.

Ibid., *Head First: The Biology of Hope*, E. P. Dutton, New York, 1989.

DeFrantz, Anita, "An Open Letter to President Bush," *New York Times*, Section 8, February 19, 1989.

Dertouzos, Michael L.; Lester, Richard K., Solow, Robert M.; and the MIT Commission on Industrial Productivity, *Made in America: Regaining the Productive Edge*, Harper Perennial div. of Harper Collins Publishers, New York, 1989.

Dubos, Rene, *Man Adapting*, Yale University Press, New Haven, 1965.

Fass, Paula, *Outside In: Minorities and the Transformation of American Education*, Oxford University Press, New York, 1989.

Fernandez, John, *Personal Interview*, August 10, 1992.

Federalist Papers, Rossiter, Clinton, ed., Penguin Books, New York, 1961.

Frankl, Victor, *Man's Search for Meaning*, Pocket Books div. of Simon and Schuster, New York, 1975.

Freund, Charles Paul, "Scandal Is A Common Top-40 Chord," *San Francisco Chronicle*, November 23, 1990, p. M1.

Gardner, John W., *Self-Renewal: The Individual and the Innovative Society*, Harper and Row Publishers, New York, 1963.

Ibid., *On Leadership*, The Free Press div. of MacMillan, Inc., New York, 1990.

Garfield, Charles, *Peak Performers: The New Heroes of American Business*, William Morrow and Co., Inc., New York, 1986.

Giamatti, A. Bartlett, *Take Time for Paradise*, Summit Books, New York, 1991.

Gibbs, Nancy, "Teens: the Rising Risk of AID, *Time*, September 2, 1991, pp. 60-61.

Goleman, Daniel, "Hope May Be Key to Success," *San Francisco Chronicle*, January 3, 1992, p. B5

Goodman, Ellen, "Contention and Continuity," *Time*, July 6, 1987, p. 57.

Ibid., "Old Friendship and Competition," *The Washington Post*, April 12, 1986, p. A-23.

Guersch, Mike, "Sports Really Are Physical Education, Teachers Say," *San Jose Mercury News,* October 3, 1990, p. E1.

Guttman, Allen, *From Ritual to Record: The Nature of Modern Sports*, Columbia University Press, New York, 1978.

Hunter-Gault, Charlayne, "Contention and Continuity," *Time*, July 6, 1987, p, 57.

Kilpatrick, William K., *Why Johnny Can't Tell Right From Wrong*, Simon and Schuster Publishers, New York, 1992.

Mandell, R. D., *Sport, A Cultural History*, Columbia University Press, New York, 1988.

Martin, Douglas, "Guiding Children To New Heights With Basketball," *New York Times,* May 7, 1989.

Mayer, J. P., ed., *Alexis de Tocqueville: Journey to America*, translated by George Lawrence, Greenwood Press, Westport, CT, 1971.

McFeaters, Ann, "Children Go Begging In America," *San Jose Mercury News*, July 3, 1991, p. B7.

Methvin, Eugene H., "The Stuff of Champions," *Readers' Digest*, October 1991, pp. 80-84.

Moore, Theresa, "Children Now Are Worse Off New Study Says," *San Francisco Chronicle*, January 3, 1992.

Murray, Charles, *In Pursuit of Happiness and Good Government*, Simon and Schuster Publishers, New York, 1989, p. 212.

National Center for Education Statistics, *National Eductional Longitudinl Study of 1988; First Follow-Up: Student Component Data File User's Manual, Vol. I*, U.S. Department of Education, Office of Educational Research and Improvement, Washington, D. C., April 1992.

Ibid., "Extracurricular Activity Participants Outperform Other Students," *Bulletin of the Office of Education Research and Improvement*, Washington, D. C., September, 1986.

Naisbitt, John, and Aburdeen, Patricia, *Re-inventing the Corporation*, Warner Books, New York, 1985.

Ibid., *Megatrends 2000*, Avon Books, New York, 1990.

Nielsen Media Research, New York, 1991.

Noddings, Nel, *The Challenge to Care in Schools: An Alternative Approach to Education,* Teachers College Press, Columbia University, New York, 1992.

Ibid., *Personal Interview*, June 28, 1992.

O'Neil, John, "A Generation Adrift," *Educational Leadership*, September 1991, pp. 4-10.

Parseghian, Ara, and Pagna, Tom, *Parseghian and Notre Dame Football*, Men-In-Motion Press, 1971.

Perez, Roberto, *Personal Interview*, February 12, 1992.

Peters, Thomas, and Waterman, Robert, *In Search of Excellence: Lesson from America's Best-Run Companies*, Harper and Row Publishers, New York, 1982.

Powers, Ron, *The Beast, the Eunuch, and the Glass-Eyed Child: Television in the '80's*, Harcourt Brace Jovanovich Publishers, New York, 1990, p. 21-39.

Ramos, Lydia, "Aiming At Dropouts, Gangs, Drugs," *San Jose Mercury News*, August 1991, p. B1.

Robinson, Tracy, *Telephone Interview*, July 4, 1992.

Rosenblatt, Roger, "Words On A Piece Of Paper," *Time*, July 6, 1987, pp. 20-21.

Salumae, Erica, *San Jose Mercury News*, January 1, 1991, p.E2.

San Jose Mercury News, May 19, 1991, p. D1.

Seligman, Martin E. P., *Helplessness: On Depression, Development, and Death*, W. H. Freeman and Co., San Francisco, 1975.

Ibid., *Learned Optimism*, Alfred A. Knopf, New York, 1991.

Shannon, Bob, *Telephone Interview*, July 8, 1992.

Spencer, James, and Barth, James, "The Deconstruction Of History In The Public School Classroom," *Social Education,* 56(1), January 1992, pp. 13-14.

Spring, Joel, *The American School 1642-1985*, Longman Publishers, New York, 1986.

Toffler, Alvin, *Future Shock*, Bantam Books, New York, 1970.

Ibid., *Power Shift*, Bantam Books, New York, 1990.

Waldon, Alton R., Jr., "Letter to the Editor," *New York Times*, June 4, 1991.

Walker, Hill, and Sylvester, Robert, "Where Is School On The Path To Prison?", *Educational Leadership*, September 1991, p. 14.

Waterman, Robert, *The Renewal Factor: How The Best Get And Keep Their Competitive Edge*, Bantam Books, New York, 1988.

Will, George, *Suddenly*, The Free Press div. of MacMillan Publishers, New York, 1990.

Women's Sports Foundation, "The Effects of Varsity Sports Participation on the Social, Educational, and Career Mobility of Minority Students," *The Women's Sports Foundation Report: Minorities in Sports*, 1989.

Wright Edelman, Maria, "Shame On The U.S.: Want To Know Our Dirty Little Secret? We Ignore Our Kids," *San Joe Mercury News*, May 19, 1991, p. C1.

Zaldivar, R. A., and Spears, Gregory, "Poverty, Apathy Put Kids In Peril," *San Jose Mercury News*, June 25, 1991, p. A1.

Index

Indiana University, 6
Individual achievement principle, 82,
    87-88, 104
    see also democratic achievement
    principle
Independence High School (San Jose,
    CA), 86
*In Search of Excellence: Lessons
    from America's Best-Run Compa
    nies* (Peters and Waterman), 81
Iowa High School Athletic Associa-
    tion, 7
Jackson, Andrew, 39
Jay, John, 59
Jefferson, Thomas, 32, 39
Johns Hopkins University, 22, 26
Johnson, Irwin "Magic", 61, 69

Kaestle, Carl F., 40
Kansas State High School Athletic
    Association, 7-8
Kennedy, John F., 45, 90, 99
Kilpatrick, William K., 19

Learning, see Leisure and learning
Leisure and
    learning, 83
    values, 82-83
Lilly Endowment, 6
Los Angeles
    South Central, 1992 riots, 11
    City Attorney's Office Gang
    Enforcement Unit, 11,111
Lundstedt, Beverly, 87, 93

MacLeish, Archibald, 96
*Made in America: Regaining the
    Competitive Edge* (Dertouzos et
    al.), 114
Madison, James, 59, 79
Mandell, R.D., 34, 38, 88
Mann, Horace, 39
Man's Search for Meaning (Frankl), 51

Maslow, Abraham, 19
Massachusetts and formal schools, 39
Mayer, J.P., 55
Meaning, sense of, 51
Mentors, need for professionally-
    trained, 14, 49
    see also Coaches
Measurable standards,
    of improvements, 57
    of performance, 57
    as modeled in co-curricular
    activities, 71
Methvin, Eugene, 74-75
Milli Vanilli, 23
Minnesota State High School League,
    7
Mission, sense of, 51
MIT Commission on Industrial
    Productivity, 81, 112
Mixed messages, 21-23, 27-28, 58,
    109
Moore, Theresa, 2
MTV, 26-27

Naisbitt, John, 96
Nation at Risk, 29
National Center for Education
    Statistics (U.S.Department of
    Education), 6-8
"National Center for Statistics
    Bulletin," 6
National Commission on Children, 2,
    18
National Commission on Excellence
    in Education, 29
National Federation of High School
    Associations, 6-8
Nazis, German, 51, 64
Nielsen Media Research, 17
Nietzsche, Friedrich, 26-27
Noddings, Nel 12-14, 67, 70, 86, 93
North Dakota High School Activities
    Association, 7